THE
COMMANDS
OF CHRIST

BROTHER EDDIE

LET THERE BE LIGHT

www.dustjacket.com

TABLE OF CONTENTS

ACKNOWLEDGEMENTS

All glory, honor, and praise to my Heavenly Father who showed me the commands, and who commissioned me to take them to every land and every language!

(✳)

SPECIAL THANKS

Dearest, my faithful wife & companion

Glenn & Katie Wrinkle

Dr. Arnold Prater

Rev. Dale Jones

Rev. Raymond Davis

Evangelist Earl Moore, my mentor

My Board of Elders & church family

Janie Lomshek, Secretary

Bob & Debbie Cole, Supporters and Cheerleaders

Special thanks to all who have contributed to my
faith journey to heaven.

RESOURCE SYMBOLS

ODB = *Our Daily Bread* devotional by RBC Ministries of Grand Rapids, MI

KMB = *Knight's Master Book of 4,000 Illustrations* by Walter Knight

Lighthouse = *The Lighthouse Devotional* compiled by Dr. Cornell Haan

Beacon = *Beacon Bible Commentary* by Beacon Hill Press of Kansas City, MO

PDL = *The Purpose Driven Life* by Rick Warren

Matthew 28:18-20 Then Jesus came and spoke to them, saying, "All authority has been given to Me in heaven and on earth. Go therefore and make disciples of all the nations, baptizing them in the name of the Father and of the Son and of the Holy Spirit, teaching them to observe all things that I have commanded you; and lo, I am with you always, even to the end of the age." Amen.

- In the Old Testament, God through the Law gave 10 commandments.

- In the New Testament, Jesus through grace and truth gave 20 commandments.

  - In the church today we are heavy on winning the lost for the Lord, but light on making disciples for Him.

  - How can we make disciples for Christ by teaching them to "observe all things that I have commanded you" unless we know what He commanded us?

  - If we do not obey Christ's Great Commission, it will become the Great Omission!

  - We must observe *all things* that He has commanded us!

  - And, we must teach others to observe all things that

He has commanded us.

- This is how we make disciples.
- This is how we obey the Great Commission."
- This is how we fulfill the Great Commission.

John 14:15 "If you love Me, keep My commandments." Revelation 22:14 Blessed are those who *do* His commandments, that they may have the right to the tree of life, and may enter through the gates into the city.

(Based on a series of 20 messages preached at Vinita, Oklahoma from February 17 - October 13, 2013)

FOREWORD

The Commands of Christ throughout the New Testament are reminders of the rules for living in everyday life.

My friend, Brother Eddie Wrinkle has written a book that focuses on right living and right thinking in a world where everything seems to be a cloudy gray.

Those who read this book will be challenged to love the scriptures and to be a faithful follower of Jesus Christ, who is the way, the truth, and the life.

Stan Toler
Bestselling Author
Oklahoma City, Oklahoma

PROLOGUE

In the church of God, I believe that we are long on soul-winning and evangelism and short on discipleship. We know how to get people saved, but we don't do such a good job discipling them or teaching them how to grow in the faith, and how to stay saved. In 2002, while I was meditating on The Great Commission in Matthew 28:18-20, the Holy Spirit led me to ask, "How can we teach others to observe all things that Christ has commanded us if we don't know how many things He commanded or what He commanded us?"

I preached the original series on The Commands of Christ at Vinita, Oklahoma from September 1, 2002 to May 18, 2003. I taught The Commands of Christ in two different conferences in India in 2004. I taught The Commands of Christ in Manila, Philippines in 2005. I most recently taught The Commands of Christ in Batticaloa, Sri Lanka, and Nasik, India, in January 2013.

Most of us know about The Ten Commandments. But most of us do not know about The Commands of Christ. We know The Ten Commandments are found in Exodus chapter 20. But most people don't know that The Commands of Christ are scattered throughout the Gospels and in the book of Revelation.

The basis of this book is to make known The Commands of Christ so that they will be taught in every land and in every language. This book is meant to be a discipleship tool and is, therefore presented in a sermon format rather than in a normal book format.

Pastors, teachers, and those who study these commands should realize that the goal of this book is to provide a "guide" to help others understand Christ's commands. Please feel free to prepare your own messages and lessons, and to use your own points, illustrations and scriptures. May the Lord be greatly glorified and may you be greatly blessed!

In Matthew 5:16 Jesus said, "Let your light so shine before men, that they may see your good works and glorify your Father in heaven."

Several years ago I wrote a Purpose Statement for my life. "My life purpose is to let the Light of Jesus shine through my life in every way possible, in every place possible, and to every person possible, for as long as possible."

LET THERE BE LIGHT!
Brother Eddie

Therefore you shall keep My commandments,
and perform them: I am the Lord. *Leviticus 22:31*

THE COMMANDS OF CHRIST #1

Seek First The Kingdom Of God And His Righteousness

Matthew 6:33 But seek first the kingdom of God and His righteousness, and all these things shall be added to you.

1. PRIORITIES ARE THE KEY

Luke 10:38-42

Now it happened as they went that He entered a certain village; and a certain woman named Martha welcomed Him into her house. And she had a sister called Mary, who also sat at Jesus' feet and heard His word. But Martha was distracted with much serving, and she approached Him and said, "Lord, do You not care that my sister has left me to serve alone? Therefore tell her to help me." And Jesus answered and said to her, "Martha, Martha, you are worried and troubled about many things. But one thing is needed, and Mary has chosen that good part, which will not be taken away from her."

One of our greatest sources of anxiety is trying to do too much. Consider how the farmer in this story might feel at the end of the day.

Early one morning a farmer tells his wife he is going to plow the "south forty." He gets off to an early start so he can oil the tractor. He needs more oil, so he goes to the shop to get it. On the way to the shop he notices the pigs weren't fed, so he proceeds to the corncrib, where he finds some sacks of feed. The sacks remind him that his potatoes are sprouting, so he heads for the potato pit. On the way there he passes the woodpile and remembers that his wife wanted firewood in the house. An ailing chicken passes as he is picking up the wood, so he puts down the wood to tend to the chicken. At the end of the day, the frustrated farmer has not even gotten to the tractor, much less the field.

Ever had a day like that? Sure! Haven't we all? So what can you do to keep from having more? You can learn to set priorities.

Martha made the *preparations* for Jesus' visit the priority, while Mary placed more importance on a *relationship* with Him. Jesus' response to Mary affirmed the importance of setting priorities.

We should pray daily about how to best use our time for the benefit of the kingdom. When we do that, we will find that there are a lot of things that just aren't as important as sitting at the Master's feet.

There is great peace in setting priorities, particularly when we ask God to show us what is most important. –

STEVE DOUGLASS
(Lighthouse – p.115)

- Part of my daily prayer is *"Order my steps and direct my paths."*
- Necessary vs. important
- Need vs. want
- We need to keep first things first, and the main thing the main thing.

<u>Phil 3:13-14</u> Brethren, I do not count myself to have apprehended; but one thing I do, forgetting those things which are behind and reaching forward to those things which are ahead, 14 I press toward the goal for the prize of the upward call of God in Christ Jesus.

- Don't let your schedule determine your priorities.
- Let your priorities determine your schedule.

"As a lighthouse for Jesus Christ, you should choose to make your relationship with Christ your top priority." – Henry Blackaby (Lighthouse – p.67)

Wouldn't it be a wonderful thing if every Christian would put loyalty to Christ above every other loyalty of life? (KMB – p.196)

- OUR PRIORITIES AT FIRST CHURCH OF GOD AT VINITA, OK ARE: *WIN...DISCIPLE...SEND!*
- DO YOU HAVE YOUR PRIORITIES STRAIGHT?

2. SEEK FIRST THE KINGDOM OF GOD

<u>Matt 6:33</u> But seek first the kingdom of God and His righteousness, and all these things shall be added to you.

- We seek first the kingdom of God through salvation!

<u>John 3:7</u> Do not marvel that I said to you, 'You must be born again.'

<u>Ps 145:13</u> Your kingdom is an everlasting kingdom, And Your dominion endures throughout all generations.

<u>Matt 4:17</u> (*Jesus' first sermon*) From that time Jesus began to preach and to say, "Repent, for the kingdom of heaven is at hand."

<u>Mark 12:34</u> (*Jesus told the scribe who came asking questions*) You are not far from the kingdom of God.

<u>Luke 11:2</u> (*Jesus taught us to pray*) Your kingdom come. Your will be done.

- Seek first the coming of the kingdom (in your heart & in the hearts of others).

- Seek first the promotion of the kingdom

- My father taught me to begin my prayers with "Thy kingdom come."

- Seek first the continuation of the kingdom.

- Are you seeing *first* the kingdom of God?

3. AND HIS RIGHTEOUSNESS

<u>Matt 6:33</u> But seek first the kingdom of God and His righteousness, and all these things shall be added to you.

- Seek His righteousness through salvation

- Seek His righteousness through sanctification

- Seek His righteousness by faith

<u>Eph 2:8-9</u> For by grace you have been saved through faith, and that not of yourselves; it is the gift of God, 9 not of works, lest anyone should boast.

<u>Isa 64:6</u> But we are all like an unclean thing, And all our righteousnesses are like filthy rags.

<u>Matt 5:20</u> For I say to you, that unless your righteousness exceeds the righteousness of the scribes and Pharisees, you will by no means enter the kingdom of heaven.

<u>Rom 3:10-12 & 23</u> As it is written,

> *"There is none righteous, no, not one;*
> *There is none who understands;*
> *There is none who seeks after God.*
> *They have all turned aside;*
> *They have together become unprofitable; There is*
> *none who does good, no, not one."*

For all have sinned and fall short of the glory of God.

2 Cor 5:21 For He made Him who knew no sin to be sin for us, that we might become the righteousness of God in Him.

Matt 5:8 Blessed are the pure in heart, For they shall see God.

Rom 14:17 for the kingdom of God is not eating and drinking, but righteousness and peace and joy in the Holy Spirit.

Heb 12:14 Pursue peace with all people, and holiness, without which no one will see the Lord:

- ARE YOU SEEKING FIRST HIS RIGHTEOUSNESS?

4. AND ALL THESE THINGS SHALL BE ADDED TO YOU

Matt 6:31-33 Therefore do not worry, saying, "What shall we eat?" or "What shall we drink?" or "What shall we wear?" For after all *these things* the Gentiles seek. For your heavenly Father knows that you need all *these things*. But seek first the kingdom of God and His righteousness, and all *these things* shall be added to you.

- Food
- Shelter
- Clothing
- If we put Christ first in all our ways, He'll supply all our needs.

<u>Phil 4:19</u> And my God shall supply all your need according to His riches in glory by Christ Jesus.

- Not our wants - but our needs.

- Proper priorities:

- Seek first the kingdom of God.

- Seek first His righteousness.

- Then *all these things* shall be added to you.

As lighthouses for Jesus Christ, our focus should be first on knowing and serving God. When we put Him first, other things fall into their rightful places. (Lighthouse – p.76)

Are you trusting Christ to provide "all these things" in their proper order?

5. J.O.Y.
(an Acrostic for Spelling JOY)

- **J**esus first
- **O**thers second
- **Y**ourself last

<u>John 15:11</u> "These things I have spoken to you, that My joy may remain in you, and that your joy may be full. "

Phil 4:4 Rejoice in the Lord always. Again I will say, rejoice!

Matt 6:33 But seek first the kingdom of God and His righteousness, and all these things shall be added to you.

- True Joy comes when our priorities are right!

CONCLUSION

Matt 6:33 But seek first the Kingdom of God and His righteousness, and all these things shall be added to you.

1. Are your priorities in proper order?
2. Are you seeking first the Kingdom God?
3. Are you seeking first his righteousness?
4. Do you trust that "All these things shall be added to you? After you have put him first
5. Do you know the way to true joy?
   Jesus
   Others
   Yourself

- The Commands of Christ lead us to salvation.

- The Commands of Christ lead us to full discipleship.

- The Commands of Christ will lead us to heaven.

John 2:5 His mother said to the servants, "Whatever He says to you, do it."

John 14:15 "If you love Me, keep My commandments."

Rev 22:14 Blessed are those who do His commandments, that they may have the right to the tree of life, and may enter through the gates into the city.

- If we do not obey Christ's Great Commission it will become the Great Omission!

- We must observe" all things" that He has commanded us!

- We must teach others to observe "all things" that He has commanded us.

- This is how we make disciples.

- This is how we create a healthy church.

- This is how we fulfill the Great Commission.

You shall not add to the word which I command you, nor take from it, that you may keep the commandments of the Lord your God which I command you. *Deuteronomy 4:2*

THE COMMANDS OF CHRIST #2

You Must Be Born Again

John 3:7 Do not marvel that I said to you, '
You must be born again.'

1. CHRIST COMMANDS US TO BE BORN AGAIN

John 3:1-7 "The New Birth"

There was a man of the Pharisees named Nicodemus, a ruler of the Jews. This man came to Jesus by night *(The original "Nick at Night")* and said to Him, "Rabbi, we know that You are a teacher come from God; for no one can do these signs that You do unless God is with him." Jesus answered and said to him, "Most assuredly, I say to you, unless one is born again, he cannot see the kingdom of God." Nicodemus said to Him, "How can a man be born when he is old? Can he enter a second time into his mother's womb and be born?" Jesus answered, "Most assuredly, I say to you, unless one is born of water and the Spirit, he cannot enter the kingdom of God. That which is born of the flesh is flesh, and that which is born of the Spirit is spirit. Do not marvel that I said to you, "You must be born again."

- John Wesley once preached the same sermon titled "You must be born again" for several weeks. The church leaders asked him why he kept preaching the same sermon. He responded – "Because *you must* be born again!"

- You must be born again if you would enter the Kingdom of God.

- You must be born again if you would enter the Church of God.

- You must be born again if you would enter heaven.

- There are two kinds of people in the world:

  1. Lost

  2. Saved

- There is only one kind of person in Heaven: Saved.

Rev 21:27 But there shall by no means enter it anything that defiles, or causes an abomination or a lie, but only those who are written in the Lamb's Book of Life.

- Did you know that fifty percent of congregations reported no conversions or baptisms in the USA last year? (2012)

- Saving the lost is God's priority. May it be ours, too!

- Christ Commands us to be Born Again."

2. THE BIBLE TELLS US HOW TO BE BORN AGAIN

John 3:4-9 – Jesus Converses with Nicodemus"
Nicodemus said to Him, "How can a man be born when he is old? Can he enter a second time into his mother's womb and be born?" Jesus answered, "Most assuredly, I say to you, unless one is born of water and the Spirit, he cannot enter the kingdom of God. That which is born of the flesh is flesh, and that which is born of the Spirit is spirit. Do not marvel that I said to you, 'You must be born again.' The wind blows where it wishes, and you hear the sound of it, but cannot tell where it comes from and where it goes. So is everyone who is born of the Spirit." Nicodemus answered and said to Him, "How can these things be?"

- Recognize the need to be born again.

- Repent of all sin

- Receive by faith–a definite time and experience

John 3:16 For God so loved the world that He gave His only begotten Son, that whoever believes in Him should not perish but have everlasting life.

Eph 2:8-9 For by grace you have been saved through faith, and that not of yourselves; it is the gift of God, not of works, lest anyone should boast.

Heb 11:6 But without faith it is impossible to please Him, for he who comes to God must believe that He is, and that He is a rewarder of those who diligently seek Him.

LIFE BETTER THAN RELIGION

Christ Jesus came into the world not to establish a religion, but to give life. In the Gospel of John the word "life" occurs forty-four times, and the word "religion" not once. Dr. Scofield once had occasion to tell a young minister that he did not believe he ever had been born again. In astonishment the young man said, "Why, I got religion ten years ago at such a place."

"That is interesting," the older minister answered; "and while you were getting religion, why didn't you get saved?"

"Why, isn't getting religion getting saved? Didn't Jesus Christ come to bring religion?"

"No. He Himself tells us why He came; 'I am come that they might have life.'"

The conversation led to the two men kneeling in prayer, and the young minister accepted Christ as his personal Saviour in a real way. (KMB – p.591)

- At Lilbourn, Missouri, the 8-12 year-olds in Vacation Bible School asked me, "How old do you have to be to get saved?" I told them, "Old enough to know that you need to be saved!"

- The Bible tells us how to be born again!

3. HAVE YOU BEEN BORN AGAIN?

- Nicodemus wasn't when he first came to Christ by night!
- But we do believe he did get saved that night.

John 7:44-52 Nicodemus Stands Up for Jesus

Now some of them wanted to take Him, but no one laid hands on Him. Then the officers came to the chief priests and Pharisees, who said to them, "Why have you not brought Him?" The officers answered, "No man ever spoke like this Man!" Then the Pharisees answered them, "Are you also deceived? Have any of the rulers or the Pharisees believed in Him? But this crowd that does not know the law is accursed." Nicodemus (he who came to Jesus by night, being one of them) said to them, "Does our law judge a man before it hears him and knows what he is doing?" They answered and said to him, "Are you also from Galilee? Search and look, for no prophet has arisen out of Galilee."

John 19:38-39 After this, Joseph of Arimathea, being a disciple of Jesus, but secretly, for fear of the Jews, asked Pilate that he might take away the body of Jesus; and Pilate gave him permission. So he came and took the body of Jesus. 39 And Nicodemus, who at first came to Jesus by night, also came, bringing a mixture of myrrh and aloes, about a hundred pounds.

- It's *Not* religion

- It's *Not* reform

- It's *Not* resolution

- But redemption that will save us!

RELIGION ISN'T SALVATION

Pandita Ramabai, the noted Christian leader of India, tells how she followed the religions of her country during her childhood days and right up until after she was married and had grown to womanhood, and of how they never satisfied. One day she heard about Christianity, and she said, *"That is what I want. Christianity will satisfy the longings of my heart. I will embrace the Christian religion."* Accepting Christianity, she sailed for England, where she was baptized and later confirmed. She joined a church in England, and for eight years lived a most exemplary Christian life. One night she happened to be listening to a message on the new birth. *Never before had she been told that she must be born again,* born from above. She was convicted, and right there and then she accepted Jesus Christ as her personal Saviour, and passed out of death into life. *This is her testimony in her own words*: "I found the Christian religion," she said, "but did not find the CHRIST of the religion." She had embraced Christianity, but she had not accepted Jesus Christ. (KMB – p.591)

Isa 1:18 "Come now, and let us reason together," Says the Lord, "Though your sins are like scarlet, They shall be as white as snow; Though they are red like crimson, They shall be as wool."

Matt 7:13-14 Enter by the narrow gate; for wide is the gate and broad is the way that leads to destruction, and there are many who go in by it. Because narrow is the gate and difficult is the way which leads to life, and there are few who find it.

2 Peter 3:9 The Lord is not slack concerning His promise, as some count slackness, but is long suffering toward us, not willing that any should perish but that all should come to repentance.

• It's a personal gospel.

Matt 27:22 Pilate said to them, "What then shall I do with Jesus who is called Christ?"

NECESSARY–AND ENOUGH

In a hospital ward, a lady missionary found an undersized and undeveloped little Irish boy, whose white, wizened face and emaciated form excited her deepest sympathy. His own soul's need was put before him, and he was awakened to some sense of his lost condition, insomuch that he commenced seriously to consider how he might be saved.

Brought up a Romanist, he thought and spoke of penance and confessional, of sacraments and church, yet never wholly leaving out Christ Jesus and His atoning work.

One morning the lady called again upon him, and found his face aglow with a new-found joy. Inquiring the reason, he replied with assurance born of faith in the revealed Word of God, "O missis, I always knew that Jesus was necessary; but I never knew till yesterday that He was enough!" (KMB – p.592)

<u>Matt 7:7-8</u> Ask, and it will be given to you; seek, and you will find; knock, and it will be opened to you. For everyone who asks receives, and he who seeks finds, and to him who knocks it will be opened.

• Have you been born again?

CONCLUSION

<u>John 3:7</u> Do not marvel that I said to you, 'You must be born again.'

1. Christ commands us to be born again.

2. The Bible tells us how to be born again.

3. Have you been born again?

WHAT THE OLD CLOCK NEEDED

A man owned a clock which he prized very highly, but one day it stopped, and he couldn't get it to go again. In order to make it work he tried different things without success. First he tried heavier weights. This, however, did not help, but rather oppressed the machinery. Then he took away the old face and put on a new one, but this made no difference. Still the clock would not go. Then he tried new hands, but this, too, failed to induce the clock to go. The owner's little boy had been an interested spectator of his father's efforts to make the clock go. At last the little boy said, "Daddy, I think the poor clock needs a new inside."

I wonder if any of you have been making good resolutions finding you cannot keep them, trying to do good, but somehow or other you have failed. Stop trying. You must begin with the New Birth. "(You) must be born again." (KMB – p.592)

- The Commands of Christ lead us to salvation.

- The Commands of Christ lead us to full discipleship.

- The Commands of Christ will lead us to heaven.

<u>John 14:15</u> If you love Me, keep My commandments.

<u>Rev 22:14</u> Blessed are those who do His commandments, that they may have the right to the tree of life, and may enter through the gates into the city.

- If we do not obey Christ's Great Commission it will become the Great Ommission!

- We must observe all things that He has commanded us!

- We must teach others to observe all things that He has commanded us.

- This is how we make disciples.

- This is how we create a healthy church.

- This is how we fulfill the Great Commission.

The statutes of the Lord are right,
rejoicing the heart; The commandment of the
Lord is pure, enlightening the eyes. *Psalm 19:8*

THE COMMANDS OF CHRIST #3

Unless Your Repent You Will All Likewise Perish

Luke 13:3 *I tell you, no; but unless you repent you will all likewise perish.*

1. WHAT REPENTANCE MEANS

Key Verse 3…unless you repent you will all likewise perish.

- One of the most important commands of Christ.

- One of the most misunderstood commands of Christ.

- One of the least obeyed commands of Christ.

- What does it mean to *repent?*

- To feel sorry, self-reproachful, or contrite for a past action, attitude, etc.; to feel remorse for sin or fault; be penitent; regret.

Isa 55:6-7 Seek the Lord while He may be found,

> *Call upon Him while He is near.*
> *Let the wicked forsake his way,*
> *And the unrighteous man his thoughts;*
> *Let him return to the Lord,*
> *And He will have mercy on him;*
> *And to our God,*
> *For He will abundantly pardon.*

- Repentance is turning from sin.
- Repentance is turning to God.

Ezek 18:20-32 the prophet told Israel to "Repent and turn from all your transgressions."

Luke 3:7-8 Then he said to the multitudes that came out to be baptized by him, "Brood of vipers! Who warned you to flee from the wrath to come? Therefore bear fruits worthy of repentance, and do not begin to say to yourselves, 'We have Abraham as our father.' For I say to you that God is able to raise up children to Abraham from these stones.'

Luke 24:46-47 Then He said to them, "Thus it is written, and thus it was necessary for the Christ to suffer and to rise from the dead the third day, and that repentance and remission of sins should be preached in His name to all nations, beginning at Jerusalem."

2 Cor 7:9-10 Now I rejoice, not that you were made sorry, but that your sorrow led to repentance. For you were made sorry in a Godly manner, that you might suffer loss from us in nothing. For

Godly sorrow produces repentance leading to salvation, not to be regretted; but the sorrow of the world produces death.

(There's A Vast Difference…Between being sorry for sin and being sorry you are "caught." KMB – p.542)

- Repentance means being sorry enough to quit.

- (Jasmin Gacoscosin told Lewis Suttee and me in October, 1992 at the Christian School in Manila, Philippines, *"Repentance means you don't do that anymore."*

REPENTANCE NECESSARY

If there is no repentance, there can be no pardon. Some years ago a murderer was sentenced to death. The murderer's brother, to whom the State was deeply indebted for former services, besought the governor of the State for his brother's pardon. The pardon was granted, and the man visited his brother with the pardon in his pocket. "What would you do,' he said to him, "if you received a pardon?"

"The first thing I would do," he answered, "is to track down the judge who sentenced me, and murder him; and the next thing I would do is to track down the chief witness, and murder him."

The brother rose, and left the prison with the pardon in his pocket. (KMB – p.542)

'Tis Not Enough
'Tis not enough to say, "I'm sorry and repent" And then go on from day to day, Just as I always went. Repentance is to leave The sins we loved before, And show that we in earnest grieve By doing them no more. (KMB – p.542)

THE DIFFERENCE BETWEEN PENANCE AND REPENTANCE

A clergyman found some children reading the Douay version of the New Testament, and on noticing a passage in the chapter which was translated "do penance" where the English version rendered the same word by "repent," *he asked them if they knew the difference between penance and repentance.* A short silence followed, and then a little girl asked, "Is it not this…: Judas did penance, and went and hanged himself; Peter repented, and wept bitterly?" (KMB – p.544)

• The Bible teaches us what repentance means!

2. WE MUST REPENT TO BECOME A CHRISTIAN

Key Verse 3…unless you repent you will all likewise perish.

<u>Rom 3:23</u> For all have sinned and fall short of the glory of God,

• Therefore, all must repent!

<u>Mark 1:14-15</u> Now after John was put in prison, Jesus came to Galilee, preaching the gospel of the kingdom of God, and saying, "The time is fulfilled, and the kingdom of God is at hand. Repent, and believe in the gospel."

<u>Mark 6:7,12</u> And He called the twelve to Himself, and began to send them out two by two, and gave them power over unclean spirits… So they went out and preached that people should repent.

<u>Luke 15:7</u> (*The Parable of the Lost Sheep*) I say to you that likewise there will be more joy in heaven over one sinner who repents than over ninety-nine just persons who need no repentance.

IMPOSSIBLE TO BE A CHRISTIAN

In a small country church, a rich man had for years been the leading elder. The congregation was looking for a new minister, and this elder interviewed each man who preached as a candidate. One of these was a truly born-again man, and his sermon was on "Repentance." Said the elder to him, "I dislike very much hearing our people called sinners."

"Are you a Christian, sir?" asked the minister. "Of course I'm a Christian," said the man.

"Then you were a sinner, and sought Christ for salvation," said the minister. "*Oh, no, I never was a sinner,*" said the elder.

"Well, sir," said the minister, "it's impossible for you to be a Christian then, because it was sinners Christ came to save. He tells us so Himself." (KMB – p.544)

<u>Mark 2:17</u> Jesus said to them, "Those who are well have no need of a physician, but those who are sick. I did not come to call the righteous, but sinners, to repentance."

<u>Rom 2:4</u> Or do you despise the riches of His goodness, forbearance, and longsuffering, not knowing that the goodness of God leads you to repentance?

- We must repent to become a Christian!

3. WE MUST REPENT TO REMAIN A CHRISTIAN

Key Verse 3…Unless you repent you will all likewise perish.

(Beacon) Even in our day it is easy, especially for church people, to point out others as sinners and in need of God's saving grace. It is not easy for one to look within and acknowledge the sin in his own heart.

1 John 2:1 My little children, these things I write to you, so that you may not sin. And if anyone sins, we have an Advocate with the Father, Jesus Christ the righteous.

- Five of the Seven churches in Asia Minor were told to repent:

    1. Rev 2:5 (*Ephesus*) Remember therefore from where you have fallen; repent and do the first works, or else I will come to you quickly and remove your lampstand from its place unless you repent.

    2. Rev 3:19 (*Laodicea*) As many as I love, I rebuke and chasten. Therefore be zealous and repent.

WHICH NEEDS HELP?

Self-righteous people know nothing of true repentance. A woman told her minister she would leave the church if a young woman who shared her pew wasn't made to occupy another seat.

Said the minister: "Madam, that girl was saved from a terrible life of sin. You say she sits and weeps quietly through the church services, and it annoys you, but it's because her heart is so full of love to her Saviour. Can't you try to understand her?"

"No, I can't," said the woman. "People who show emotion over their religion annoy me. *I have always lived a good life. I don't make any fuss.*"

"Well, madam," said the minister, "have a talk with the girl; I believe she can help you." (KMB – p.544)

- WE MUST REPENT TO REMAIN A CHRISTIAN!

4. WE MUST REPENT OR PERISH

Key Verse 3...unless you repent you will all likewise perish.

(Beacon) On the one hand Jesus was at least implying that calamity was not necessarily a direct punishment for sin. On the other hand He was specifically pointing out that, apart from the grace of God, all are sinners and that all sinners will perish unless they repent.

...To all who have sinned (and all have sinned) Jesus says, Except ye repent, ye shall all likewise perish. And the calamity of these Galileans cannot be compared with the calamity of hell.

Or those eighteen, upon whom the tower in Siloam fell... (4). The fact that Jesus uses this event to strengthen His argument would strongly imply that the people knew well the particulars of the case and that the men who were killed in the fall of the tower were not notably wicked men but average Jewish workmen.

I tell you, Nay: but except ye repent, ye shall all likewise perish (5). Jesus repeats verse 3 verbatim for emphasis. The truth He was teaching was most significant – important enough to call forth this repetition. Even in our day it is easy, especially for church people, to point out others as sinners and in need of God's saving grace. It is not easy for one to look within and acknowledge the sin in his own heart. (Beacon)

John 3:16 For God so loved the world that He gave His only begotten Son, that whoever believes in Him should not perish but have everlasting life.

- Unless you all repent, you will go to hell!

Matt 11:20-22 Then He began to rebuke the cities in which most of His mighty works had been done, because they did not repent: 21 "Woe to you, Chorazin! Woe to you, Bethsaida! For if the mighty works which were done in you had been done in Tyre and Sidon, they would have repented long ago in sackcloth and ashes. 22 But I say to you, it will be more tolerable for Tyre and Sidon in the day of judgment than for you."

1 Peter 3:9 The Lord is not slack concerning His promise, as some count slackness, but is longsuffering toward us, not willing that any should perish but that all should come to repentance.

- We must repent or perish!

CONCLUSION

<u>Luke 13:3</u> I tell you, no; but unless you repent you will all likewise perish."

1. Do you know what it means to repent?

2. Have you repented in order to become a Christian?

3. Have you committed sins as a Christian that need to be repented of?

4. Do you know you will perish in hell unless you repent?

IT BROKE HIM DOWN

Dr. Evans, when a student at Moody Bible Institute, began talking to a man at the Pacific Garden Mission, about his soul. The man argued: "I do not believe the Bible. I am an atheist." Evans repeated one verse, "Except you repent, you shall all likewise perish." The fellow scoffed, "I told you I didn't believe it."

Again Evans quoted, "Except you repent, you shall all likewise perish." The man exasperatingly uttered, "You disgusting fellow, what is the use of telling me that?"

Again Evans repeated the verse. In anger, the man struck Dr. Evans between the eyes with his fist, sending the Bible one way and Evans the other. God gave him grace. He got up and said, "My friend, God loves you, and 'except you repent, you shall all likewise perish.'"

The next night that man was in the mission before the meeting began. He confessed: "I could not sleep. All over the wall I read, 'Except you repent, you shall all likewise perish.' I saw it on my pillow. When I got up I saw 'Except you repent,' at the breakfast table, and all through the day it was before me. I have come back to settle it." (KMB – p.543)

Acts 26:19-20 "Therefore, King Agrippa, I was not disobedient to the heavenly vision, 20 but declared first to those in Damascus and in Jerusalem, and throughout all the region of Judea, and then to the Gentiles, that they should repent, turn to God, and do works befitting repentance."

Repent and Turn
Repent and turn! God calls today; Oh, do not close
thine ear, I pray! Listen! It is the Voice of love–
Grieve not that tender heart above.

Repent and turn! Now is the hour, The time of
God's redeeming power; Tomorrow it may be too
late. Just now wide open is the gate.

Repent and turn! Christ shed His blood To reconcile
thy soul to God! All has been done; for refuge flee,
Apply the Blood, He'll pass o'er thee.

As when the ancient Israelite, Upon that dark
Egyptian night, Put on his door the mark of blood,
And so escaped the wrath of God.

My friend, I plead, do thou the same– Put all thy
trust in Jesus' Name! Not all good works, nor prayers
of thine, Can save apart from Blood Divine.

But that will save! Before Him bow Repent
and turn and trust Him now.

For soon will end the day of grace:
God's wrath is coming on apace.

<u>Luke 13:3</u> I tell you, no; but unless you repent you will all like-
wise perish.

He who keeps the commandment keeps his soul,
But he who is careless of his ways will die.
Proverbs 19:16

THE COMMANDS OF CHRIST #4

Receive the Holy Spirit

John 20:22 And when He had said this, He breathed on them,
and said to them, "Receive the Holy Spirit."

Acts 1:4-5

And being assembled together with them, He commanded them not to depart from Jerusalem, but to wait for the Promise of the Father, "which," He said, "you have heard from Me; 5 for John truly baptized with water, but you shall be baptized with the Holy Spirit not many days from now."

1. HE COMMANDED THEM

John 20:22 And when He had said this, He breathed on them, and said to them, "Receive the Holy Spirit."

<u>Acts 1:4</u> He commanded them to wait for the promise of the father.

(Beacon) The term found here is used "especially of the transmitted orders of a military commander." The disciples were not yet adequately equipped for their major offensive against the enemy. So their General issued the order that they were to wait (lit., "remain around") until empowered by the Holy Spirit for carrying out their commission. (Beacon)

- Jesus commanded them to receive the Holy Spirit.

- Jesus commanded them not to depart from Jerusalem until they had received the Holy Spirit.

- Jesus commanded them to wait for the promise of the Father.

<u>Luke 24:49</u> "Behold, I send the Promise of My Father upon you; but tarry in the city of Jerusalem until you are endued with power from on high."

<u>1 Thess 4:3-4,7-8</u> For this is the will of God, your sanctification: that you should abstain from sexual immorality; 4 that each of you should know how to possess his own vessel in sanctification and honor, 7 For God did not call us to uncleanness, but in holiness. 8 Therefore he who rejects this does not reject man, but God, who has also given us His Holy Spirit.

2. YOU SHALL BE BAPTIZED WITH THE HOLY SPIRIT

John 20:22 And when He had said this, He breathed on them, and said to them, "Receive the Holy Spirit."

Acts 1:5 For John truly baptized with water, but you shall be baptized with the Holy Spirit not many days from now.

(Beacon) This strong emphasis on the baptism with the Holy Spirit, as being greater and more essential than the baptism with water, anticipates the central thrust of the Book of Acts. *Any Christianity that neglects the Spirit-baptism is incomplete and pre-Pentecost.* Actually, it has not yet caught up with the preaching of John the Baptist. Without this baptism there would have been no Book of Acts, and in fact no Church of Jesus Christ today. Without the baptism of the Holy Spirit in personal experience there is no adequate enablement for victorious living and effective service.

DIFFERENT TERMS FOR SANCTIFICATION

- Spirit-filled, Holiness, Second work of grace, Second blessing, Deeper walk with God, Second touch, Inner Light etc.

- Different meanings for baptized with the Holy Spirit

- Endued, clothed, poured on, immersed in, fell upon, filled, anointed…etc.

Luke 3:16 John answered, saying to all, "I indeed baptize you with water; but One mightier than I is coming, whose sandal strap I am not worthy to loose. He will baptize you with the Holy Spirit and <u>fire</u>."

- Fire purifies

- Fire empowers

- Fire illuminates

Acts 2:36-41 "Therefore let all the house of Israel know assuredly that God has made this Jesus, whom you crucified, both Lord and Christ." Now when they heard this, they were cut to the heart, and said to Peter and the rest of the apostles, "Men and brethren, what shall we do?" Then Peter said to them, "Repent, and let every one of you be baptized in the name of Jesus Christ for the remission of sins; and you shall receive the gift of the Holy Spirit. For the promise is to you and to your children, and to all who are afar off, as many as the Lord our God will call." And with many other words he testified and exhorted them, saying, "Be saved from this perverse generation." Then those who gladly received his word were baptized; and that day about three thousand souls were added to them.

Acts 1:5 For John truly baptized with water, but you shall be baptized with the Holy Spirit not many days from now."

- You can be baptized with the Holy Spirit.

- You should be baptized with the Holy Spirit.

- You shall be baptized with the Holy Spirit.

- They did and we can too!

<u>Acts 2:1-4</u> When the Day of Pentecost had fully come, they were all with one accord in one place. And suddenly there came a sound from heaven, as of a rushing mighty wind, and it filled the whole house where they were sitting. Then there appeared to them divided tongues, as of fire, and one sat upon each of them. And they were all filled with the Holy Spirit and began to speak with other tongues, as the Spirit gave them utterance.

3. YOU SHALL RECEIVE POWER

<u>Acts 1:6-8</u> Therefore, when they had come together, they asked Him, saying, "Lord, will You at this time restore the kingdom to Israel?" And He said to them, "It is not for you to know times or seasons which the Father has put in His own authority. But you shall receive power when the Holy Spirit has come upon you; and you shall be witnesses to Me in Jerusalem, and in all Judea and Samaria, and to the end of the earth."

- *Authority*: see Matthew 28:18

(Beacon) Power should be "authority." The Greek word is not <u>dynamis</u>, as in verse 8, but exousia. Properly this means: "freedom to exercise the inward force or faculty expressed by <u>dynamis</u>," and so "right" or "authority." <u>Dynamis </u>implies "the possession of the ability to make power felt," whereas <u>exousia </u>"affirms that free movement is ensured to the ability."

Acts 1:8 is the key verse of this significant book. It gives at once both the *power* and the *program* of the Church of Jesus Christ. The <u>power </u>is the Holy Spirit. The <u>program is</u> the evangelization of the world. *For a person to claim to be filled with the Spirit and yet not to be vitally concerned about world missions is to deny his profession.* When the Holy Spirit fills the human heart with his power and presence, He generates the urge to carry out Christ's command. The converse is also true: the Great Commission cannot be fulfilled without the power of the Spirit.

The Greek word for power, as already noted, is *dynamis* (cf. "dynamite," "Dynamo"). This means "power, might, strength, force." It here signifies "that power, especially is connected with their office of witnessing to the resurrection; but also all other spiritual power."

The first clause of this verse states clearly that *power comes when the Holy Spirit comes.* This is because He is power. There is no spiritual power apart from the presence of the Spirit of God. That is why every Christian needs to be filled with the Spirit.

- Moral power
- Spiritual power
- Witnessing power
- Jesus was saying to His Disciples: "You don't have this power now, but you shall."

<u>Acts 4:31,33</u> And when they had prayed, the place where they were assembled together was shaken; and they were all filled with the Holy Spirit, and they spoke the word of God with boldness. 33 And with great power the apostles gave witness to the resurrection of the Lord Jesus. And great grace was upon them all.

- The Holy Spirit gives us the power to be, see, say, stay. *(Dr. O.L. Johnson)*

4. YOU SHALL BE WITNESSES

<u>Acts 1:8</u> "But you shall receive power when the Holy Spirit has come upon you; and you shall be witnesses to Me in Jerusalem, and in all Judea and Samaria, and to the end of the earth."

- Witnesses at Jerusalem

- Witnesses in Judea and Samaria

- Witnesses to the end of the earth (the end of life…the end of time)

The word witnesses (singular and plural) occurs thirteen times in Acts. (Beacon)

- Jesus told his disciples to go.

- Jesus told his disciples to make disciples.

- Jesus told his disciples to do this in the power of the Holy Spirit.

- The Holy Spirit would give them the power to promote Christ and His kingdom, not self!

<u>Matt 5:16</u> Let your light so shine before men, that they may see your good works and glorify your Father in heaven.

- Witnesses: Peter, Stephen, Paul, Corrie ten Boom, D.L. Moody…etc.

<u>Luke 24:45-48</u> And He opened their understanding, that they might comprehend the Scriptures. Then He said to them, "Thus it is written, and thus it was necessary for the Christ to suffer and to rise from the dead the third day, and that repentance and

remission of sins should be preached in His name to all nations, beginning at Jerusalem. And you are witnesses of these things."

- We are to be witnesses, not judges
- Not lawyers
- We are to see and tell

Acts 5:32 And we are His witnesses to these things, and so also is the Holy Spirit whom God has given to those who obey Him.

CONCLUSION

John 20:22 And when He had said this, He breathed on them, and said to them, "Receive the Holy Spirit."

Acts 1:4-5 And being assembled together with them, He commanded them not to depart from Jerusalem, but to wait for the Promise of the Father, "which," He said, "you have heard from Me; 5 for John truly baptized with water, but you shall be baptized with the Holy Spirit not many days from now."

1. He commanded them. Have you obeyed?
2. You shall be baptized with the Holy Spirit. Have you been?
3. You shall receive power. Have you received power?
4. You shall be witnesses. Are you His witness?

HOW TO BE SANCTIFIED:

1. YOU MUST BE SAVED

   John 14:16-17 And I will pray the Father, and He will give you another Helper, that He may abide with you forever — 17 the Spirit of truth, whom the world cannot receive, because it neither sees Him nor knows Him; but you know Him, for He dwells with you and will be in you.

2. YOU MUST RECOGNIZE YOUR NEED

3. YOU MUST CONSECRATE

   Rom 12:1 I beseech you therefore, brethren, by the mercies of God, that you present your bodies a living sacrifice, holy, acceptable to God, which is your reasonable service.

   • Consecration means to take a blank sheet of paper & sign your name at the bottom. Then ask the Lord to fill in the rest. (*Bro. Raymond Davis*)

4. YOU MUST ASK

   Luke 11:13 If you then, being evil, know how to give good gifts to your children, how much more will your heavenly Father give the Holy Spirit to those who ask Him!

5. YOU MUST RECEIVE

   Acts 19:1-2 And it happened, while Apollos was at Corinth, that Paul, having passed through the upper regions, came to Ephesus. And finding some disciples he said to them, "Did you receive the Holy Spirit when you believed?"

Eph 5:18 Be filled with the Spirit.

WAVES OF LIQUID LOVE!

In his writings, Charles G. Finney says, "He who neglects to obey the command to be filled with the Spirit, is as guilty of breaking the command of God, as he who steals, or curses, or commits adultery. His guilt is as great as the authority of God is great, who commands us to be filled. His guilt is equivalent to all the good he might do if he were filled with the Spirit." (KMB – p.287)

1 Thess 5:23-24 Now may the God of peace Himself sanctify you completely; and may your whole spirit, soul, and body be preserved blameless at the coming of our Lord Jesus Christ. He who calls you is faithful, who also will do it.

Heb 12:14 Pursue peace with all people, and holiness, without which no one will see the Lord:

Heb 13:12 Therefore Jesus also, that He might sanctify the people with His own blood, suffered outside the gate.

John 20:22 And when He had said this, He breathed on them, and said to them, "Receive the Holy Spirit."

Let us hear the conclusion of the whole matter:
Fear God and keep His commandments,
For this is man's all. *Ecclesiastes 12:13*

THE COMMANDS OF CHRIST #5

Follow Me and I Will Make You Fishers of Men

Matthew 4:19 Then He said to them, "Follow Me, and I will make you fishers of men."

During World War II, B-17 bombers made long flights from the US mainland to the Pacific island of Saipan. When they landed there, the planes were met by a jeep bearing the sign: "Follow Me!" That little vehicle guided the giant planes to their assigned places in the parking area.

One pilot, who by his own admission was not a religious man, made an insightful comment: "That little jeep with its quaint sign always reminds me of Jesus. He was [a lowly] peasant, but the giant men and women of our time would be lost without His direction." (ODB – 3.5.03)

1. FOLLOW ME

<u>Matt. 4:18-19</u> And Jesus, walking by the Sea of Galilee, saw two brothers, Simon called Peter, and Andrew his brother, casting a net into the sea; for they were fishermen. 19 Then He said to them, "Follow Me."

Matthew 17:1-8

Now after six days Jesus took Peter, James, and John his brother, led them up on a high mountain by themselves; and He was transfigured before them. His face shone like the sun, and His clothes became as white as the light. And behold, Moses and Elijah appeared to them, talking with Him. Then Peter answered and said to Jesus, "Lord, it is good for us to be here; if You wish, let us make here three tabernacles: one for You, one for Moses, and one for Elijah." While he was still speaking, behold, a bright cloud overshadowed them; and suddenly a voice came out of the cloud, saying, "This is My beloved Son, in whom I am well pleased. Hear Him!" And when the disciples heard it, they fell on their faces and were greatly afraid. But Jesus came and touched them and said, "Arise, and do not be afraid." When they had lifted up their eyes, they saw no one but Jesus only.

- Don't follow Moses
- Don't follow Elijah
- Don't follow John the Baptist
- Don't follow Luther
- Don't follow Wesley
- Don't follow a religion – Catholic or Protestant
- Jesus said, "Follow Me!"

John 21:18-22 Jesus at the Sea of Galilee *(3ʳᵈ appearance)*

"Most assuredly, I say to you, when you were younger, you girded yourself and walked where you wished; but when you are old, you will stretch out your hands, and another will gird you and carry you where you do not wish." *This He spoke, signifying by what death he would glorify God.* And when He had spoken this, He said to him, "Follow Me." Then Peter, turning around, saw the disciple whom Jesus loved following, who also had leaned on His breast at the supper, and said, "Lord, who is the one who betrays You?" Peter, seeing him, said to Jesus, *"But Lord, what about this man?"* Jesus said to him, "If I will that he remain till I come, what is that to you? You follow Me."

FOLLOW ME TO SALVATION

John 14:6 Jesus said to him, "I am the way, the truth, and the life. No one comes to the Father except through Me."

Acts 4:12 "Nor is there salvation in any other, for there is no other name under heaven given among men by which we must be saved."

- No other way.
- No other name.

FOLLOW ME TO SELF-DENIAL

Luke 9:23-26 Then He said to them all, "If anyone desires to come after Me, let him deny himself, and take up his cross daily, and follow Me. For whoever desires to save his life will lose it, but whoever loses his life for My sake will save it. For what profit is it to a man if he gains the whole world, and is himself destroyed or lost? For whoever is ashamed of Me and My words, of him the Son of Man will be ashamed when He comes in His own glory, and in His Father's, and of the holy angels."

1 Peter 2:21 For to this you were called, because Christ also suffered for us, leaving us an example, that you should follow His steps:

- He shed His blood.
- He gave His life.
- He took our place.

Matthew 26:39,42,44... three times Jesus prayed in Gethsemane, "Not My will but Yours be done."

- What we admire in Jesus - self denial - is sorely needed in us!

FOLLOW ME TO SERVICE

- Matt. 4:19 Then He said to them, "Follow Me, and I will make you fishers of men."

- A call and a command

Matt 20:25-28 (*The other ten were indignant after James and John's mother asked for greatness for her two sons*)

But Jesus called them to Himself and said, "You know that the rulers of the Gentiles lord it over them, and those who are great exercise authority over them. Yet it shall not be so among you; but whoever desires to become great among you, let him be your servant. And whoever desires to be first among you, let him be your slave — 28 just as the Son of Man did not come to be served, but to serve, and to give His life a ransom for many."

- There are many who desire to be leaders, but not many who desire to be servants.

- There are many books and videos on leadership, but not many on servanthood.

- Unless you're a good servant, you won't make a good leader!

FOLLOW ME TO SAFETY

<u>John 16:33</u> These things I have spoken to you, that in Me you may have peace. In the world you will have tribulation; but be of good cheer, I have overcome the world.

<u>Rev 21:3-4</u> And I heard a loud voice from heaven saying, "Behold, the tabernacle of God is with men, and He will dwell with them, and they shall be His people. God Himself will be with them and be their God. And God will wipe away every tear from their eyes; there shall be no more death, nor sorrow, nor crying. There shall be no more pain, for the former things have passed away."

- There is no safety in this world apart from Jesus.

- We'll never be truly safe until we get to heaven.

- When I was a boy of about 14, there was a close play at home plate. When I scored, my mother yelled from the stands, "Safe as in the arms of Jesus!"

- When I slide across home plate someday, I hope I'll hear those words.

2. AND

Matt. 4:19 Then He said to them, "Follow Me, and…"

- There's more to being a Christian than getting saved.
- There's more to following Jesus than getting others baptized.
- There's an "and" involved in this command.
- Many miss this "and."
- Certainly Jesus calls us to follow Him to Salvation, Self-denial, Service, and Safety.
- But He doesn't wish the following to stop there.
- So He puts an "and" to show there's more to this command.
- There's something else to follow.

3. I WILL MAKE YOU FISHERS OF MEN

Matt. 4:19 Then He said to them, "Follow Me, and I will make you fishers of men."

- **Win**
- **Disciple**
- **Send**
- Jesus is looking for availability.
- Jesus will show you *how* to fish for men.
- Jesus will show you *when* to fish for men.

- Jesus will show you *where* to fish for men.
- Jesus will make you "*fishers of men.*"

Luke 5:1-11

So it was, as the multitude pressed about Him to hear the word of God, that He stood by the Lake of Gennesaret, and saw two boats standing by the lake; but the fishermen had gone from them and were washing their nets. 3 Then He got into one of the boats, which was Simon's, and asked him to put out a little from the land. And He sat down and taught the multitudes from the boat. When He had stopped speaking, He said to Simon, "Launch out into the deep and let down your nets for a catch." But Simon answered and said to Him, "Master, we have toiled all night and caught nothing; *nevertheless at Your word I will let down the net.*" And when they had done this, they caught a great number of fish, and their net was breaking. So they signaled to their partners in the other boat to come and help them. And they came and filled both the boats, so that they began to sink. When Simon Peter saw it, he fell down at Jesus' knees, saying, "Depart from me, for I am a sinful man, O Lord!" For he and all who were with him were astonished at the catch of fish which they had taken; and so also were James and John, the sons of Zebedee, who were partners with Simon. And Jesus said to Simon, "Do not be afraid. From now on you will catch men." So when they had brought their boats to land, they forsook all and followed Him.

John 21:1-7

After these things Jesus showed Himself again to the disciples at the Sea of Tiberias, and in this way He showed Himself: Simon Peter, Thomas called the Twin, Nathanael of Cana in Galilee, the sons of Zebedee, and two others of His disciples were together. Simon Peter said to them, "I am going fishing." They said to him, "We are going with you also." They went out and immediately got into the boat, and that night they caught nothing. But when the morning had now come, Jesus stood on the shore; yet the disciples did not know that it was Jesus. Then Jesus said to them, "Children, have you any food?" They answered Him, "No." And He said to them, "Cast the net on the right side of the boat, and you will find some." So they cast, and now they were not able to draw it in because of the multitude of fish. Therefore that disciple whom Jesus loved said to Peter, "It is the Lord!."

- At a fraternity house at Louisiana Tech in Ruston, God used me to catch George Dean plus three families for Him.

- In Manila October 2010, God used me to catch four hundred children for Him at the Christian School.

Matt 9:36-38 But when He saw the multitudes, He was moved with compassion for them, because they were weary and scattered, like sheep having no shepherd. Then He said to His disciples, "The harvest truly is plentiful, but the laborers are few. Therefore pray the Lord of the harvest to send out laborers into His harvest."

"Reaching the lost is God's priority. May it be ours, too!"

"I will make you fishers of men, fishers of men, fishers of men;
I will make you fishers of men if you follow Me.
If you follow Me; If you follow Me.
I will make you fishers of men if you follow Me."

CONCLUSION

<u>Matthew 4:19</u> Then He said to them, "Follow Me, and I will make you fishers of men."

- Once a man followed mother plus us four kids across town as we drove to our father's grocery store. When we asked him why he was following us, he told us, "Your bumper sticker says, follow me to Wrink's Market."

- Jesus says:
  Follow Me to salvation
  Follow Me to self-denial
  Follow Me to service
  Follow Me to safety

1. Are you following Jesus?
2. Are you open and obedient to the *And*?
3. Are you a fisher of men?

Centuries after our Savior walked the streets and hills of Israel, the world with all its advances still needs His example and instruction. When His ways aren't followed, numerous problems and evils arise in our world—including immorality, crime, and greed.

How do we follow Jesus' ways? First of all, we turn from our sin and entrust our lives to Him as our Savior and Lord. Then, we seek His will in His Word each day and put it into practice by the power of the Holy Spirit within us. We learn to deny our selfish desires and give ourselves completely to following Jesus.

If you want to get in line with the purposes of God, respond to Jesus' invitation: "Follow Me!" (ODB – 3.5.03)

TO FIND YOUR WAY THROUGH LIFE, FOLLOW JESUS

John 10:27 My sheep hear My voice, and I know them, and they follow Me.

Rev 14:1-4 Then I looked, and behold, a Lamb standing on Mount Zion, and with Him one hundred and forty-four thousand, having His Father's name written on their foreheads. And I heard a voice from heaven, like the voice of many waters, and like the voice of loud thunder. And I heard the sound of harpists playing their harps. They sang as it were a new song before the throne, before the four living creatures, and the elders; and no one could learn that song except the hundred and forty-four thousand who were redeemed from the earth. These are the ones who were not defiled with women, for they are virgins. These are the ones who follow the Lamb wherever He goes. These were redeemed from among men, being firstfruits to God and to the Lamb.

- At a Paducah, Kentucky campground, there was a picture that showed a flock of sheep following Jesus up a narrow trail.

John 14:15 If you love Me, keep My commandments.

Rev 22:14 Blessed are those who do His commandments, that they may have the right to the tree of life, and may enter through the gates into the city.

And I prayed to the Lord my God, and made confession,
and said, "O Lord, great and awesome God, who keeps
His covenant and mercy with those who love Him,
and with those who keep His commandments. *Daniel 9:4*

THE COMMANDS OF CHRIST #6

Go Therefore and Make Disciples of All the Nations

Matthew 28:19 Go therefore and make disciples of all the nations, baptizing them in the name of the Father and of the Son and of the Holy Spirit.

"Discipleship—the process of becoming like Christ— always begins with a decision. <u>Jesus calls us, and we respond</u>: "Come, be my disciple," Jesus said to him. So Matthew got up and followed him. - *Matt. 9:9 NLT* (The Purpose Driven Life – p.179 by Rick Warren)

1. THE DECISION TO GO

v.19...Go therefore and make disciples of all the nations, baptizing them in the name of the Father and of the Son and of the Holy Spirit,

- Someone asked, "What's the 'therefore' there for?"

- In this case, it's because Jesus has "All authority in heaven and on earth." (v.18)

- Since Jesus has "All authority in heaven and on earth," He *therefore* commands to "Go and make disciples of all the nations."

- We are commanded to "go" in the authority given to us by Jesus.

- I wonder if we would've gone if He hadn't commanded us to.

- Many are going many places and doing many things, but not for the Lord.

- "Many talk of going on pilgrimage who never go." *(Pilgrim's Progress by John Bunyan)*

Matt 21:28-31 *(The Parable of the Two Sons)* "But what do you think? A man had two sons, and he came to the first and said, 'Son, go, work today in my vineyard.' He answered and said, 'I will not,' but afterward he regretted it and went. Then he came to the second and said likewise. And he answered and said, 'I go, sir,' but he did not go. Which of the two did the will of his father?" They said to Him, "The first."

IT BEGINS WITH A DECISION

Luke 14:15-24 *"The Parable of the Great Supper"*

Now when one of those who sat at the table with Him heard these things, he said to Him, "Blessed is he who shall eat bread in the kingdom of God!" Then He said to him, "A certain man gave a great supper and invited many, and sent his servant at supper time to say to those who were invited, 'Come, for all things are now ready.' But they all with one accord began to make excuses. The first said to him, 'I have bought a piece of ground, and I must go and see it. I ask you to have me excused.' And another said, 'I have bought five yoke of oxen, and I am going to test them. I ask you to have me excused.' Still another said, 'I have married a wife, and therefore I cannot come.' So that servant came and reported these things to his master. Then the master of the house, being angry, said to his servant, 'Go out quickly into the streets and lanes of the city, and bring in here the poor and the maimed and the lame and the blind.' And the servant said, 'Master, it is done as you commanded, and still there is room.' Then the master said to the servant, 'Go out into the highways and hedges, and compel them to come in, that my house may be filled. For I say to you that none of those men who were invited shall taste my supper.'"

- The Commands of Christ
- They're not going to come in on their own.
- We're going to have to go out and invite/compel them to come in.
- Have you decided to go?

2. THE DECISION TO MAKE DISCIPLES

v.19…Go therefore and make disciples of all the nations, baptizing them in the name of the Father and of the Son and of the Holy Spirit,

After the command to *go* Jesus does not leave us without direction as to what we're to do.

- First, we need to *be* a disciple.

- Then we need to *go* and make other disciples.

- It takes time.

- It takes effort.

- Salvation is a crisis experience

- Discipleship is a lifetime experience

- <u>Disciple</u>: 1. Believer 2. Follower 3. Learner

- It's one thing to win them.

- It's another thing to disciple them.

- [*The old saying*] "If you give a man a fish you can feed him for a day. But, if you teach him how to fish, he can feed his family for many days."

- HAVE YOU DECIDED TO HELP MAKE DISCIPLES?

2. THE DECISION TO BAPTIZE

v.19…Go therefore and make disciples of all the nations, baptizing them in the name of the Father and of the Son and of the Holy Spirit.

- First, you need to be saved and baptized.

- The Disciples/Pastors *the ordained/called leaders* are to baptize.

But every Christian can help in this area by making sure their children and grandchildren are baptized, as well as others.

Baptism is not an optional ritual, to be delayed or postponed. *It signifies your inclusion in God's family.* It publicly announces to the world, "I am not ashamed to be a part of God's family," HAVE YOU BEEN BAPTIZED? *Jesus commanded this beautiful act for all in his family…*

For years I wondered why Jesus' Great Commission gives the same prominence to baptism as it does to the great tasks of evangelism and edification. Why is baptism so important? Then I realized it is because it symbolized…participating in the fellowship of God's eternal family.

Baptism is pregnant with meaning. *Your baptism declares your faith, shares Christ's burial and resurrection, symbolized your death to your old life, and announces your new life in Christ.* It is also a celebration of your inclusion in God's family.

Your baptism is a physical picture of a spiritual truth. It represents what happened the moment God brought you into His family: "Some of us are Jews, some are Gentiles, some are slaves, and some are free. But we have all been baptized into Christ's body by one Spirit, and we have all received the same Spirit."

Baptism doesn't make you a member of God's family; only faith in Christ does that. Baptism shows you are part of God's family. *Like a wedding ring, it is a visible reminder of an inward commitment made in your heart.* It is an act of initiation… not something you put off until you are spiritually mature. The only biblical condition is that you believe. (*The Purpose Driven Life pp.120-121 by Rick Warren*)

- There are no delayed baptisms in the New Testament. Most, if not all baptisms in the New Testament occurred on the same day people were saved.

- If you've been saved, do not delay to be baptized as soon as possible.

- If you're in ministry, do not delay to baptize converts as soon as possible.

- Have you decided to obey this command?

4. THE DECISION TO TEACH

Key Verse 20…Teaching them to observe all things that I have commanded you; and lo, I am with you always, even to the end of the age." Amen.

- *This is how we make disciples.* We teach them to observe all the things that Christ has commanded us.

- How can we "make disciples of all the nations" by teaching them to "observe all things that (CHRIST) commanded (us)" unless we know what He commanded us?

- Knowing how many commands there are is important!

- Then we need to obey the commands and teach others to obey them.

<u>1 Cor 12:28</u> lists teaching as one of the gifts of the Spirit.

<u>Eph 4:11</u> lists teachers as one of the gifts of Christ to the church.

<u>John 6:11</u> And Jesus took the loaves, and when He had given thanks He distributed them to the disciples, and the disciples to those sitting down; and likewise of the fish, as much as they wanted.

- Teachers are distributers–they take what Christ has blessed and broken and distribute it to others.

<u>Acts 8:1-4</u> Now Saul was consenting to (*Stephen's*) death. At that time a great persecution arose against the church which was at Jerusalem; and they were all scattered throughout the regions of Judea and Samaria, except the apostles. And devout men carried Stephen to his burial, and made great lamentation over him. As for Saul, he made havoc of the church, entering every house, and dragging off men and women, committing them to prison. Therefore those who were scattered went everywhere preaching (*teaching*) the word.

<u>2 Tim 2:1-2</u> You therefore, my son, be strong in the grace that is in Christ Jesus. And the things that you have heard from me among many witnesses, commit these to faithful men who will be able to teach others also.

<u>2 Tim 2:24-25</u> And a servant of the Lord must not quarrel but be gentle to all, able to teach, patient, in humility correcting those who are in opposition, if God perhaps will grant them repentance, so that they may know the truth.

<u>Heb 5:12</u> For though by this time you ought to be teachers, you need someone to teach you again the first principles of the oracles of God; and you have come to need milk and not solid food.

<u>James 3:1</u> My brethren, let not many of you become teachers, knowing that we shall receive a stricter judgment.

- **Have you decided to teach The Commands of Christ?**

CONCLUSION

<u>Matt 28:19</u> Go therefore and make disciples of all the nations, baptizing them in the name of the Father and of the Son and of the Holy Spirit,

1. Have you decided to go?
2. Have you decided to make disciples?
3. Have you decided to be baptized and to baptize?
4. Have you decided to teach?

<u>Isa 6:8-9</u> Also I heard the voice of the Lord, saying:

> *"Whom shall I send, And who will go for Us?"*
> *Then I said, "Here am I! Send me." 9 And He said,*
> *"Go, and tell this people…"*

HOW ARE YOU TREATING
The Great Commission?

- Have you gone?
- Are you going?

- Will you go?

IT'S IN YOUR HANDS

Two brothers were arguing about the wisdom of their parents. "Father is very wise," said the first brother. "We should listen to him and do what he says." The second brother disagreed. "Father is not so wise! Why, we are just as smart as he is. I'll prove it to you!"

The next day the second brother went into the woods near his home and captured a small bird. He brought the bird home and said to his brother, "Let's go find our father. I will show you that he isn't so smart!"

The two brothers went into their father's study, the second one holding the small bird between his cupped hands. "Father, I have a question for you," he said. "I hold a small bird in my hands. Tell me, is this bird dead or alive? *The boy was confident that his father would not answer correctly because if he said that the bird was dead, the boy would simply open his hands and show that the bird was alive. If his father answered that the bird was alive, he would crush the bird between his hands and reveal that the bird was dead.* Then he would prove to his brother that this father was not so wise after all. The boys' father considered the question for a moment and said, "My son...the answer is in your hands."

Whoever therefore breaks one of the least of these commandments, and teaches men so, shall be called least in the kingdom
of heaven; but whoever does and teaches them, he shall be
called great in the kingdom of heaven.
Matthew 5:19

THE COMMANDS OF CHRIST #7

Love One Another; As I Have Loved You

John 13:34 *A new commandment I give to you, that you love one another; as I have loved you, that you also love one another.*

- This was the text from my first sermon – 9.23.1973 (a.m.) at the Park Manor Church of God, Lebanon, MO.

1. A NEW COMMANDMENT

Vvs.34-35 A new commandment I give to you, that you love one another; as I have loved you, that you also love one another. By this all will know that you are My disciples, if you have love for one another."

- A new level of love.
- A new kind of love.

(Beacon) *The command of love for one's neighbor was not new* (Lev. 19:18; Luke 10:27). But to love...as I have loved you–that was new! Our Lord's love reached to a Judas (13:5,26) who would betray Him, and a Peter who would deny Him, *In fact this kind of love was an event so unique that a new verbal vehicle had to be devised to express it.* The eros (not in NT) of the Greeks described only selfish love; and philia (in NT only Jas. 4:4) described no more than the friendship love that thinks in terms of getting as well as giving. *But the selfless sacrifice of Jesus, His willingness to give all without any guarantee of human response, had to be expressed in a stronger word.* So agape, a rare word for LOVE prior to Paul, came to be used in early Christian literature to describe the kind of love that Jess demonstrated, and the quality of love that is to character-ize the lives of His true disciples.

Matthew 5:43-48 Love Your Enemies

"You have heard that it was said, 'You shall love your neighbor and hate your enemy.' *But I say to you, love your enemies, bless those who curse you, do good to those who hate you, and pray for those who spitefully use you and persecute you,* that you may be sons of your Father in heaven; for He makes His sun rise on the evil and on the good, and sends rain on the just and on the unjust. For if you love those who love you, what reward have you? Do not even the tax collectors do the same? And if you greet your brethren only, what do you do more than others? Do not even the tax collectors do so? Therefore you shall be perfect, just as your Father in heaven is perfect."

1 Corinthians 13:1-8 Love Never Fails

If I speak in the tongues of men and of angels, but have not love, I am only a resounding gong or a clanging cymbal. If I have the gift of prophecy and can fathom all mysteries and all knowledge, and if I have a faith that can move mountains, but have not love, I am nothing. If I give all I possess to the poor and surrender my body to the flames, but have not love, I gain nothing. Love is patient, love is kind. It does not envy, it does not boast, it is not proud. It is not rude, it is not self-seeking, it is not easily angered, it keeps no record of wrongs. Love does not delight in evil but rejoices with the truth. It always protects, always trusts, always hopes, always perseveres. Love never fails.

1 Cor 13:13 And now abide faith, hope, love, these three; but the greatest of these is love.

NO FAREWELL TO LOVE

As an aged Christian lay dying in Edinburgh, a friend called to say farewell. "I have just had three other visitors," said the dying man, "and with two of them I parted; but the third I shall keep with me forever."

"Who are they?"

"*The first was Faith,* and I said, 'Goodbye, Faith! I thank God for your company ever since I first trusted Christ; but now I am going where faith is lost in sight.' *Then came Hope.* 'Farewell, Hope!' I cried. 'You have helped me in many an hour of battle and distress, but now I shall not need you, for I am going where hope passes into fruition.' Last of all came Love. 'Love,' said I, 'you have indeed been my friend; you have linked me with God and with my fellow men; you have comforted and gladdened all my pilgrimage. But I cannot leave you behind; you must come with me through the gates, into the city of God, for love is perfected in heaven.'" (KMB – p.399)

2. LOVE ONE ANOTHER AS I HAVE LOVED YOU

Vvs.34-35 A new commandment I give to you, that you love one another; as I have loved you, that you also love one another. 35 By this all will know that you are My disciples, if you have love for one another."

- How did Jesus love us?

John 13:1 Now before the Feast of the Passover, when Jesus knew that His hour had come that He should depart from this world to the Father, having loved His own who were in the world, He loved them to the end.

John 15:12-14 This is My commandment, that you love one another as I have loved you. Greater love has no one than this, than to lay down one's life for his friends. You are My friends if you do whatever I command you.

Rom 5:6-8 For when we were still without strength, in due time Christ died for the ungodly. For scarcely for a righteous man will one die; yet perhaps for a good man someone would even dare to die. But God demonstrates His own love toward us, in that while we were still sinners, Christ died for us.

Eph 5:25-29 Husbands, love your wives, just as Christ also loved the church and gave Himself for her, that He might sanctify and cleanse her with the washing of water by the word, that He might present her to Himself a glorious church, not having spot or wrinkle or any such thing, but that she should be holy and without blemish. So husbands ought to love their own wives as their own bodies; he who loves his wife loves himself. For no one ever hated his own flesh, but nourishes and cherishes it, just as the Lord does the church.

1 John 4:10,19 In this is love, not that we loved God, but that He loved us and sent His Son to be the propitiation for our sins. We love Him because He first loved us.

Romans 8:35-39

Who shall separate us from the love of Christ? Shall tribulation, or distress, or persecution, or famine, or nakedness, or peril, or sword? As it is written:

> *"For Your sake we are killed all day long; We are*
> *accounted as sheep for the slaughter."*

Yet in all these things we are more than conquerors through Him who loved us. For I am persuaded that neither death nor life, nor angels nor principalities nor powers, nor things present nor things to come, nor height nor depth, nor any other created thing, shall be able to separate us from the love of God which is in Christ Jesus our Lord.

Prov 10:12 Hatred stirs up strife, But love covers all sins.

LOVE COVERS

I received a fine letter from a friend in Switzerland. It is difficult for him to write in English, and he naturally was aware of some unique usages of the language. However, he made it all seem very beautiful as he ended with the sentence, "The mistakes you will cover with the coat of love." <u>How necessary it is that we have that great love in our hearts toward our friends!</u> We all make so many mistakes in life! Our real friends always seem to understand because they cover our mistakes with their love. (KMB – p.400)

- Are you a sin-coverer or re-caller?

> *To walk in love with saints above*
> *Will be a wondrous glory;*
> *But to walk below with saints you know—*
> *Well, that's another story!*

<u>Rom 5:5</u> Now hope does not disappoint, because the love of God has been poured out in our hearts by the Holy Spirit who was given to us. (*Corrie ten Boom's favorite Bible verse*)

- To "love as I have loved you" requires that our hearts be filled with *His* love.

- It is the Holy Spirit who enables us to love as Christ loved us!

<u>1 Peter 1:22-23</u> Since you have purified your souls in obeying the truth through the Spirit in sincere love of the brethren, love one another fervently with a pure heart, 23 having been born again, not of corruptible seed but incorruptible, through the word of God which lives and abides forever,

3. BY THIS ALL WILL KNOW THAT YOU ARE MY DISCIPLES

Vvs.34-35 A new commandment I give to you, that you love one another; as I have loved you, that you also love one another. 35 By this all will know that you are My disciples, if you have love for one another."

- Not by tongues, Not by works, Not by gifts, Not by sermons, Not by Sunday School lessons, Not by musical talent, Not by religion, BUT BY THE LOVE OF CHRIST FOR ONE ANOTHER shall all men know that we are His disciples.

It is by a love like this, Jesus said, that all men shall know that ye are my disciples, if ye have love one to another (35). Mac-Gregor says: *"There is to be a new love-circle, the Christian Church, dependent upon a new love-centre, Christ."* He then quotes Tertullian as saying: "The heathen are wont to exclaim with wonder, See how these Christians love one another." (Beacon)

Gal 6:10 Therefore, as we have opportunity, let us do good to all, especially to those who are of the household of faith.

1 John 3:10-14 In this the children of God and the children of the devil are manifest: Whoever does not practice righteousness is not of God, nor is he who does not love his brother. For this is the message that you heard from the beginning, that we should love one another, not as Cain who was of the wicked one and murdered his brother. And why did he murder him? Because his works were evil and his brother's righteous. Do not marvel, my

brethren, if the world hates you. We know that we have passed from death to life, because we love the brethren. He who does not love his brother abides in death.

- After Russell Frala was saved at Lilbourn, Missouri, he received a new kind of love for the people of the congregation. They all looked different to him.

- When Lewis Suttee was saved at Vinita, Oklahoma, he thought something had happened to the people in the congregation. In reality, it had happened to him.

1 John 4:20-21 If someone says, "I love God," and hates his brother, he is a liar; for he who does not love his brother whom he has seen, how can he love God whom he has not seen? And this commandment we have from Him: that he who loves God must love his brother also.

- If you cannot love a Christian brother or sister, neither will you love a sinner!

- If you cannot love a Christian brother or sister, you cannot be a Christian!

CONCLUSION

John 13:34 A new commandment I give to you, that you love one another; as I have loved you, that you also love one another.

1. He gave us a "new commandment"...have we kept it?

2. He told us to love one another as He loved us…have we done it?

3. He said by this all will know that we are his disciples… can they tell?

LOVE IN ACTION

Dr. C.H. Parkhurst has a chapter in his book, *Love as a Lubricant*, in which he relates this little story: One day there was a workman aboard a trolley car, and he noticed that every time the door was pushed open it squeaked. Rising from his seat, he took a little can from his pocket, and dropped oil on the offending spot. He sat down again, quietly remarking, "*I always carry an oil can in my pocket, for there are so many squeaky things that a drop of oil will correct.*" Love is the oil which alone can make everyday life in home and business and society harmonious. (KMB – p.399)

- Is there someone you don't love?
- Christ loves them, and He can help you love them?
- You cannot be his disciple if you do not love one another!

1 John 4:7-8,11,18 Beloved, let us love one another, for love is of God; and everyone who loves is born of God and knows God… He who does not love does not know God, for God is love…11 Beloved, if God so loved us, we also ought to love one another…18 There is no fear in love; but perfect love casts out fear, because fear involves torment. But he who fears has not been made perfect in love.

PERFECT LOVE

Slow to suspect–quick to trust,
Slow to condemn–quick to justify,
Slow to offend–quick to defend,
Slow to expose–quick to shield,
Slow to reprimand–quick to forbear,
Slow to belittle–quick to appreciate,
Slow to demand–quick to give,
Slow to provoke–quick to conciliate,
Slow to hinder–quick to help,
Slow to resent–quick to forgive.
(KMB – p.400)

• (The Burkeville, Texas revival, August 1983) There was a woman and her uncle who hadn't spoken to each other in a year. During the invitation she went to him and asked for his forgiveness.

Luke 11:28 Blessed are those who hear the word of God and keep it!

But why do you call Me "Lord, Lord," and not do the things which I say? *Luke 6:46*

THE COMMANDS OF CHRIST #8

Whoever Desires to Come After Me, Let Him Deny Himself

Mark 8:34 When He had called the people to Himself, with His disciples also, He said to them, "Whoever desires to come after Me, let him deny himself, and take up his cross, and follow Me."

1. WHOEVER DESIRES TO COME AFTER ME

v.34…When He had called the people to Himself, with His disciples also, He said to them, "*Whoever* desires to come after Me,

John 3:16 *Whoever* believes in Him should not perish but have everlasting life.

Rev 22:17 *Whoever* desires, let him take the water of life freely.

- Do you really desire to follow Jesus?

- Many speak of going on pilgrimage who never go. (John Bunyan)

<u>Luke 14:28</u> For which of you, intending to build a tower, does not sit down first and count the cost, whether he has enough to finish it.

- There's a cost in following Jesus.
- There's a cost in *not* following Jesus!
- Have you counted the cost?

WHERE DOES JESUS GO?

<u>Matt 15:24</u>... "I was sent to the lost sheep of the house of Israel."

<u>Mark 2:17</u> "Those who are well have no need of a physician, but those who are sick. I did not come to call the righteous, but sinners, to repentance."

<u>Luke 14:21-23</u> "Go out quickly into the streets and lanes of the city, and bring in here the poor and the maimed and the lame and the blind." And the servant said, 'Master, it is done as you commanded, and still there is room.' 23 Then the master said to the servant, "Go out into the highways and hedges, and compel them to come in, that my house may be filled."

- Jesus would go into the jails, nursing homes, hospitals and broken homes...
- He would minister to the dying, to the suffering, and the sorrowing.
- He would serve. He would work. etc.
- OR It's not an easy of glamorous path to come after Jesus!

2. LET HIM DENY HIMSELF

Vv.34-35...Whoever desires to come after Me, let him deny himself, and take up his cross, and follow Me. For whoever desires to save his life will lose it, but whoever loses his life for My sake and the gospel's will save it.

These days we hear a lot about self-confidence, self - expression, self-satisfaction, self-effort, and selfishness, but not much about *self denial*!

Matt 10:37-39 He who loves father or mother more than Me is not worthy of Me. And he who loves son or daughter more than Me is not worthy of Me. And he who does not take his cross and follow after Me is not worthy of Me. He who finds his life will lose it, and he who loses his life for My sake will find it.

- Are you willing to deny yourself houses or lands, fame or position?

- Are you willing to deny yourself wealth or comfort in order to come after Jesus?

Matt 6:33 But seek first the kingdom of God and His righteousness, and all these things shall be added to you.

Matt 10:39 He who finds his life will lose it, and he who loses his life for My sake will find it.

FINDING LIFE BY LOSING IT

The story is told of Sundar Singh who was traveling with a Tibetan companion on a bitterly cold day. Snow was falling heavily, and both men were almost too frozen to go forward; they felt they would never survive the terrible experience. They reached a steep precipice, and there they saw that a man had slipped over the edge, and was lying, almost dead, on the ledge of rock below. *Sundar suggested that they should carry the poor fellow into safety.* The Tibetan refused to help, saying it was all they could do to save themselves; and he went on, leaving Sundar behind. *With great difficulty the Sadhu managed to get the dying man up the slope and on to his back, and then he struggled on with his heavy burden.* Before long he came upon the body of his former companion, the Tibetan. He was dead, frozen to death. *On struggled Sundar, and gradually the dying man, receiving warmth from the friction of his own body against that of his rescuer, began to revive, while the Sadhu himself grew warm through his labor.* At last they reached a village and were safe. With a full heart, Sundar thought of the words of his Master: "Whoever will save his life shall lose it; and whoever will lose his life for My sake shall find it." (KMB – p.617)

Luke 14:26 If anyone comes to Me and does not hate his father and mother, wife and children, brothers and sisters, yes, and his own life also, he cannot be My disciple.

John 12:24-25 Most assuredly, I say to you, unless a grain of wheat falls into the ground and dies, it remains alone; but if it dies, it produces much grain. He who loves his life will lose it, and he who hates his life in this world will keep it for eternal life.

John 15:13 Greater love has no one than this, than to lay down one's life for his friends.

Rom 12:1 I beseech you therefore, brethren, by the mercies of God, that you present your bodies a living sacrifice, holy, acceptable to God, which is your reasonable service.

WHEN SELF GETS IN THE WAY

"Some of us are so full of ourselves…that we cannot see Christ in all His beauty." Some years ago, when (the father) was away on a preaching appointment, (his) wife and little daughter stayed at the home of a friend. On the bedroom wall, just over the head of the bed in which they slept there was a picture of the Lord Jesus, which was reflected in the large mirror of the dressing table standing in the bay of the bedroom window. When the little daughter woke on her first morning there, she saw the picture reflected in the mirror while she still lay in bed, and exclaimed, "Oh, Mommy, I can see Jesus through the mirror?"

Then she quickly kneeled up to take a better look, but in doing do brought her own body between the picture and the mirror, so that instead of seeing the picture of Jesus reflected, she now saw herself. So she lay down again, and again she saw the picture of Jesus. She was up and down several times after that with her eyes fixed on the mirror. Then she said, "Mommy, when I can't see myself, I can see Jesus; but every time I see myself, I don't see Him." How true it is when self fills the vision, we do not see Jesus. (KMB – pp.613-614)

A Christian is an odd number anyway. He feels supreme love for One that he's never seen; Talks familiarly every day to Someone he cannot see; Expects to go to heaven on the virtue of Another; Empties himself in order to be full; Admits that he is wrong so that he can be declared right; Goes down in order to get up; Is the strongest when he's the weakest; Richest when he's the poorest; Happiest when he feels the worst; He dies so he can live; Forsakes in order to have; Gives away so he can keep; Sees the invisible, Hears the inaudible, and Knows that which passes understanding. (A.W. Tozer)

3. AND TAKE UP HIS CROSS

V.34 Whoever desires to come after Me, let him deny himself, and take up his cross.

- Many are willing to wear the crown without bearing the cross.

- We each have a cross to bear!

- Jesus says that if we desire to follow Him, we will have a life of suffering, sorrow, and self-denial.

- Luke 9:23 Then He said to them all, "If anyone desires to come after Me, let him deny himself, and take up his cross daily, and follow Me."

- Our cross is that which we suffer due to following Jesus:

- Persecution, loss of family, friends, jobs, affliction that comes as a direct or indirect result of serving Jesus, etc.

Gal 6:14 But God forbid that I should boast except in the cross of our Lord Jesus Christ, by whom the world has been crucified to me, and I to the world.

- Sanctification is not so much an outer manifestation as an inner crucifixion. (*Bro. Earl Moore*)

AND SAILED THROUGH BLOODY SEAS!

Do not be indifferent to this thing called Christianity. It was created for you by the blood of Christ and preserved for you by the blood of the martyrs.

For almost the first three hundred years Christianity was a forbidden thing. Its adherents were publicly whipped, dragged by their heels through the streets until their brains ran out. Their limbs were torn off, their ears and noses were cut off, and their eyes were dug out with sharp sticks or burned out with hot irons. Sharp knives were run under their finger nails. Melted lead was poured over their bodies. They were drowned, beheaded, crucified, ground between stones, torn by wild beasts, smothered in lime kilns, scraped to death by sharp shells, and killed all day long.

In 1651 in Massachusetts, Rev. Obadiah Holmes, because he held a prayer meeting in his home, was ordered to be whipped by Governor Endicot. So severe was the whipping that for days he could lie only by resting on the tips of his elbows and his knees and yet when the last lash had fallen, he looked at his tormenters and through bloodstained lips cried, "Gentlemen, you have whipped me with roses!"

A redeeming Christ has given you a future filled with hope. Do not look lightly upon this thing called Christianity, which cost the Son of God His blood, and millions of His followers their lives. (KMB – pp.586-587)

HOW THE APOSTLES DIED

All of the apostles were insulted by the enemies of their Master. They were called to seal their doctrines with their blood and nobly did they bear the trial.

Matthew suffered martyrdom by being slain with a sword at a distant city of Ethiopia. Mark expired at Alexandria, after being cruelly dragged through the streets of that city. Luke was hanged upon an olive tree in the classic land of Greece. John was put in a caldron of boiling oil, but escaped death in a miraculous manner, and was afterward branded at Patmos. (He was the only Apostle *not* to die a martyr's death.).) Peter was crucified at Rome with his head downward. James, the Greater, was beheaded at Jerusalem. James, the Less, was thrown from a lofty pinnacle of the temple, and then beaten to death with a fuller's club. Bartholomew was flayed alive. Andrew was bound to a cross (in the shape of an X), whence he preached to his persecutors until he died. Thomas was run through the body with a lance (in India). Jude was shot to death with arrows. Matthias was first stoned and then beheaded. Barnabas was stoned to death at Salonica. Paul, after various tortures and persecutions, was at length beheaded at Rome by the Emperor Nero. Such was the fate of the apostles, according to traditional statements. (KMB – p.587)

MUST JESUS BEAR THE CROSS ALONE
by Thomas Shepherd

Must Jesus bear the cross alone, And all the world go free? No; there's a cross for everyone, And there's a cross for me.

4. AND FOLLOW ME

Key verse 34…Whoever desires to come after Me, let him deny himself, and take up his cross, and follow Me.

- A disciple is a believer.

- A disciple is a learner.

- A disciple is a follower.

Matt 4:19 Then He said to them, "Follow Me, and I will make you fishers of men."

John 8:12 Then Jesus spoke to them again, saying, "I am the light of the world. He who follows Me shall not walk in darkness, but have the light of life."

John 10:27 My sheep hear My voice, and I know them, and they follow Me.

Luke 9:57-62

Now it happened as they journeyed on the road, that someone said to Him, "Lord, I will follow You wherever You go." And Jesus said to him, "Foxes have holes and birds of the air have nests, but the Son of Man has nowhere to lay His head." Then He said to another, "Follow Me." But he said, "Lord, let me first go and bury my father." Jesus said to him, "Let the dead bury their own dead, but you go and preach the kingdom of God." 61 And another also said, "*Lord, I will follow You*, but let me first go and bid them farewell who are at my house." 62 But Jesus said to him, "No one, having put his hand to the plow, and looking back, is fit for the kingdom of God."

- (Hymn) "Wherever He leads, I'll go"
- (Hymn) "Follow, follow, I will follow Jesus"

Rev 14:4 These are the ones who follow the Lamb wherever He goes. These were redeemed from among men, being firstfruits to God and to the Lamb.

CONCLUSION

<u>Mark 8:34</u> When He had called the people to Himself, with His disciples also, He said to them, "Whoever desires to come after Me, let him deny himself, and take up his cross, and follow Me."

1. Whoever desires to come after Me

2. Let him deny himself

3. And take up his cross

4. And follow Me

IS IT TRUE SELF-DENIAL?

One morning, as Harry and his parents were sitting at the breakfast table, Harry seemed to be for a while engaged in deep study. Presently he exclaimed, "Father, I have made up my mind not to eat any more salt mackerel."

"Ah, what has brought you to that conclusion?" asked his father, with a look of earnest inquiry. *"Because,"* continued Harry, *"My Sunday School teacher said that we ought to give up something so that we might have money to put in the missionary box."* "Well, but what has induced my boy to choose salt mackerel as the thing he will give up?" asked his father. "Why," answered Harry, "because mackerel doesn't come very often; and I don't like it very much anyhow." Have there been some older folk who have tried to practice self- denial in about the same way? (KMB – p.616)

DEATH TO SELF

In a city he visited during one of his many journeys preaching the Word of God, (a preacher) noticed a sign in a small establishment (that dyed garments) which read:

"I Live To Dye, I Dye To Live
The More I Dye The More I Live
The More I Live The More I Dye..."

...The more there is death to self, that much more fully is the Lord Jesus Christ able to live His life in us. "I am crucified with Christ; nevertheless I live; yet not I, but Christ liveth in me" (Gal. 2:20). *This kind of living is possible to every believer by full appropriation of all that is his in Christ.* "Likewise reckon yourselves to be dead indeed unto sin, but alive unto God through Jesus Christ our Lord." (Rom. 6:11). (KMB – p. 612)

<u>John 14:15</u> If you love Me, keep My commandments.

<u>Rev 22:14</u> Blessed are those who do His commandments, that they may have the right to the tree of life, and may enter through the gates into the city.

His mother said to the servants,
"Whatever He says to you, do it." *John 2:5*

THE COMMANDS OF CHRIST #9

If You Have Anything Against Anyone, Forgive Him

Mark 11:25 And whenever you stand praying, if you have anything against anyone, forgive him, that your Father in heaven may also forgive you your trespasses.

1. A DIRECT COMMAND

Key Verse 25… "And whenever you stand praying, if you have anything against anyone, forgive him,"

- No ifs, ands, or buts
- Not implied nor hinted at
- No loopholes or options
- Not a suggestion.
- Jesus didn't say "Begin to forgive." He said, "Forgive."

John 14:15 If you love Me, keep My commandments.

John 15:14 You are My friends *if* you do whatever I command you.

Rev 22:14 Blessed are those who *do* His commandments, that they may have the right to the tree of life, and may enter through the gates into the city.

2. UNLESS YOU FORGIVE

Vvs.25-26…"And whenever you stand praying, if you have anything against anyone, forgive him, that your Father in heaven may also forgive you your trespasses. 26 But if you do not forgive, neither will your Father in heaven forgive your trespasses."

Matthew 18:21-35

Then Peter came to Him and said, "Lord, how often shall my brother sin against me, and I forgive him? Up to seven times?" Jesus said to him, "I do not say to you, up to seven times, but up to seventy times seven. Therefore the kingdom of heaven is like a certain king who wanted to settle accounts with his servants. And when he had begun to settle accounts, one was brought to him who owed him ten thousand talents. But as he was not able to pay, his master commanded that he be sold, with his wife and children and all that he had, and that payment be made. The servant therefore fell down before him, saying, 'Master, have patience with me, and I will pay you all.' Then the master of that servant was moved with compassion, released him, and forgave him the debt.

"But that servant went out and found one of his fellow servants who owed him a hundred denarii; and he laid hands on him and took him by the throat, saying, 'Pay me what you owe!' So his fellow servant fell down at his feet and begged him, saying, 'Have patience with me, and I will pay you all.' And he would not, but went and threw him into prison till he should pay the debt. So when his fellow servants saw what had been done, they were very grieved, and came and told their master all that had been done. Then his master, after he had called him, said to him, 'You wicked servant! I forgave you all that debt because you begged me. Should you not also have had compassion on your fellow servant, just as I had pity on you?' And his master was angry, and delivered him to the torturers until he should pay all that was due to him. "So My heavenly Father also will do to you if each of you, from his heart, does not forgive his brother his trespasses."

- Edward Beisly said "It's easy for me to forgive."

BOTH NEEDED THE GRACE OF GOD

A shamefaced employee was summoned to the office of the senior partner to hear his doom. The least that he could expect was a blistering dismissal; he might even be sent to prison for years. The old man called his name and asked him if he were guilty. The clerk stammered out that he had no defense.

"I shall not send you to prison," said the old man. "If I take you back, can I trust you?"

When the surprised and broken clerk had given assurance and was about to leave, the senior partner continued: "You are the second man who has fallen and been pardoned, in this business. I was the first. What you have done, I did. The mercy you have received, I received. It is only the grace of God that can keep us both." (KMB – p.229)

- John Wesley once encountered a man who said that he could not forgive someone for what they had done to him. Wesley said, "Then you had better not sin from now on!"
- You cannot be a disciple of Jesus unless you forgive..
- You cannot remain a disciple of Jesus unless you forgive.

3. FORGIVE AS CHRIST FORGAVE YOU
FREELY–WHETHER THEY ASK OR NOT

Matthew 5:43-48 Love Your Enemies

You have heard that it was said, "You shall love your neighbor and hate your enemy." But I say to you, love your enemies, bless those who curse you, do good to those who hate you, and pray for those who spitefully use you and persecute you, that you may be sons of your Father in heaven; for He makes His sun rise on the evil and on the good, and sends rain on the just and on the unjust. For if you love those who love you, what reward have you? Do not even the tax collectors do the same? And if you greet your brethren only, what do you do more than others? Do not even the tax collectors do so? Therefore you shall be perfect, just as your Father in heaven is perfect.

Luke 7:41-43 "There was a certain creditor who had two debtors. One owed five hundred denarii, and the other fifty. And when they had nothing with which to repay, he freely forgave them both. Tell Me, therefore, which of them will love him more?" Simon answered and said, "I suppose the one whom he forgave more." And He said to him, "You have rightly judged."

- Jesus forgave us freely from the cross.

Eph 4:30-32 And do not grieve the Holy Spirit of God, by whom you were sealed for the day of redemption. Let all bitterness, wrath, anger, clamor, and evil speaking be put away from you, with all malice. And be kind to one another, tenderhearted, forgiving one another, even as God in Christ forgave you.

Col 3:12-13 Therefore, as the elect of God, holy and beloved, put on tender mercies, kindness, humility, meekness, long suffering; bearing with one another, and forgiving one another, if anyone has a complaint against another; even as Christ forgave you, so you also *must* do.

WHAT CHRIST HAD DONE FOR HER

The wife of a Zulu chief attended a Salvation Army meeting and heard and responded to the call of Jesus. When her husband heard of this he forbade her to go again on pain of death. However, eager to hear more about Jesus, she dared to go, and when her husband knew of this he met her on her return journey and beat her so savagely that he left her for dead. By and by his curiosity moved him to go back and look for her. She was not where he had left her, but he found her lying under a bush. *Covering her with his cruel eyes he leered, "And what can your Jesus Christ do for you now?"*

She opened her eyes, and looking at him, said gently, "He helps me to forgive you!" (KMB – p.228)

WHICH PLACE WILL YOU TAKE?

"Doing an injury puts you below your enemy; revenging one makes you but even with him; forgiving it sets you above him." – Benjamin Franklin (KMB – p.230)

4. A MATTER OF OBEDIENCE

- Not feelings.

- "Forgiveness is not based on emotions, but is an act of the will."

- Corrie ten Boom and the guard from Ravensbruck–how she saw him several years after World War II and she struggled to forgive him after he asked her. She asked the Lord to give her the strength to forgive. The Lord supplied the feelings after she forgave him.

Jer 7:23-24 But this is what I commanded them, saying, Obey My voice, and I will be your God, and you shall be My people. And walk in all the ways that I have commanded you, that it may be well with you. Yet they did not obey or incline their ear, but followed the counsels and the dictates of their evil hearts, and went backward and not forward.

Matt 5:23-24 Therefore if you bring your gift to the altar, and there remember that your brother has something against you, leave your gift there before the altar, and go your way. First be reconciled to your brother, and then come and offer your gift.

<u>Matt 7:21</u> "Not everyone who says to Me, 'Lord, Lord,' shall enter the kingdom of heaven, but he who does the will of My Father in heaven."

<u>1 Peter 1:22</u> Since you have purified your souls in obeying the truth through the Spirit in sincere love of the brethren, love one another fervently with a pure heart,

<u>Acts 24:16</u> (*Paul told Felix*) "This being so, I myself always strive to have a conscience without offense toward God and men."

- *Nike* says "Just do it"
- "Even those in covenant relationship with God can expect His blessing only when they are obedient to His laws and commandments."

CONCLUSION

<u>Mark 11:25</u> And whenever you stand praying, if you have anything against anyone, forgive him, that your Father in heaven may also forgive you your trespasses.

1. Do you know Christ has commanded us to forgive?
2. Do you know that unless you forgive you cannot be forgiven?
3. Do you know that you must forgive as Christ forgave you?
4. Do you know that forgiveness is a matter of obedience not feelings?

- Is there anyone you need to forgive today?

- Do you need to be forgiven?

- What if they won't forgive you? Then, it's their problem.

- If you won't forgive others, then it's your problem.

WHY REVIVAL WAS BLOCKED

(*D.L. Moody once said*) I remember one town that Mr. Sankey and myself visited. *For a week it seemed as if we were beating the air; there was no power in the meetings.* At last, one day, I said that perhaps there was someone cultivating the unforgiving spirit. The chairman of our committee, who was sitting next to me, got up and left the meeting right in view of the audience. The arrow had hit the mark, and gone home to the heart of the chairman of the committee. He had had trouble with someone for about six months. *He at once hunted up this man and asked him to forgive him.* He came to me with tears in his eyes, and said: "I thank God you ever came here." That night the inquiry-room was thronged. The chairman became one of the best workers I have ever known, and he has been active in Christian service ever since. (KMB – p.231)

THERE MUST BE NO BITTERNESS

Madame Chiang Kai-shek's Christian words admonish us: "There must be no bitterness in the reconstructed world. No matter what we have undergone and suffered, we must try to forgive those who have injured us, and to remember only the lessons we have gained thereby."

Booker T. Washington once said, "I am determined to permit no man to narrow or degrade my soul by making me hate him." (KMB – p.233)

<u>Heb 12:14-15</u> Pursue peace with all people, and holiness, without which no one will see the Lord: looking carefully lest anyone fall short of the grace of God; lest any root of bitterness springing up cause trouble, and by this many become defiled;

<u>Jas 5:9</u> Do not grumble against one another, brethren, lest you be condemned. Behold, the Judge is standing at the door!

- We all need forgiveness!
- We all need to forgive!
- If you would be forgiven, you *must* forgive.
- If you would be Christ's disciple, you *must* forgive.
- Wipe the slate clean.

Matthew 6:9-13 The Lord's Prayer

In this manner, therefore, pray:

> *Our Father in heaven,*
> *Hallowed be Your name.*
>
> *Your kingdom come.*
>
> *Your will be done On earth as it is in heaven.*
>
> *Give us this day our daily bread.*
>
> *And forgive us our debts,*
>
> *As we forgive our debtors.*
>
> *And do not lead us into temptation,*
>
> *But deliver us from the evil one.*
>
> *For Yours is the kingdom and the*
>
> *power and the glory forever.*
>
> *Amen.*

- You can't pray the Lord's prayer with hate in your heart.
- You cannot pray the Lord's prayer without forgiving.

If you love Me, keep My commandments. *John 14:15*

THE COMMANDS OF CHRIST #10

Men Always Ought To Pray And Not Lost Heart

Luke 18:1 Then He spoke a parable to them, that men always ought to pray and not lose heart.

KEY TRUTH

Prayer is God's chosen way of communication and fellowship between the Christian and Himself. It is the secret of spiritual growth and effective service. "Prayer is like breathing, in the life of a Christian."

(Sunday school lesson – 2.2.03 The Christian and Prayer)

1. WE ALWAYS OUGHT TO PRAY

v.1…Then He spoke a parable to them, that men always ought to pray and not lose heart,

- WE = Men and women, boys and girls "ought always to pray - Every Day!

- Whether we feel good or bad.

- Whether we feel like it or not.

- Whether things go well or bad.

- Prayer should be our first resort—not our last!

Luke 18:2-8 Parable of the Woman & the Judge

There was in a certain city a judge who did not fear God nor regard man. Now there was a widow in that city; and she came to him, saying, "Get justice for me from my adversary." And he would not for a while; but afterward he said within himself, "Though I do not fear God nor regard man, yet because this widow troubles me I will avenge her, lest by her continual coming she weary me." Then the Lord said, "Hear what the unjust judge said. 7 And shall God not avenge His own elect who cry out day and night to Him, though He bears long with them? I tell you that He will avenge them speedily. Nevertheless, when the Son of Man comes, will He really find faith on the earth?"

Ps 55:17 Evening and morning and at noon I will pray, and cry aloud, And He shall hear my voice.

Dan 6:10 Now when Daniel knew that the writing was signed, he went home. And in his upper room, with his windows open toward Jerusalem, he knelt down on his knees three times that day, and prayed and gave thanks before his God, as was his custom since early days.

Rom 12:12 Rejoicing in hope, patient in tribulation, continuing steadfastly in prayer;

1 Thess 5:17 pray without ceasing,

- If we pray without ceasing, we'll never cease to pray. (*Bro. Moore – revival at Vinita – 4.5.1994*)

- We ought always to pray!

2. WE OUGHT NEVER TO LOSE HEART

v.1…Then He spoke a parable to them, that men always ought to pray and not lose heart.

- The devil wants to discourage us..
- The devil wants us to give up.
- The devil wants us to lose heart.

Hab 3:17-18 Though the fig tree may not blossom, Nor fruit be on the vines; Though the labor of the olive may fail, And the fields yield no food; Though the flock may be cut off from the fold, And there be no herd in the stalls—Yet I will rejoice in the Lord, I will joy in the God of my salvation.

Matt 26:41 "Watch and pray, lest you enter into temptation. The spirit indeed is willing, but the flesh is weak."

Heb 10:23 Let us hold fast the confession of our hope without wavering, for He who promised is faithful.

- "Never Give Up!" (Churchill's famous speech)

- Never give up praying.

- Never give up hoping.

- Never give up trusting.

- Never give up your faith in God.

- We ought never to lose heart!

3. CHRIST TAUGHT US TO PRAY

<u>Luke 11:1</u> Now it came to pass, as He was praying in a certain place, when He ceased, that one of His disciples said to Him, "Lord, teach us to pray, as John also taught his disciples."

Matthew 6:5-13 "The Lord's Prayer"

And when you pray, you shall not be like the hypocrites. For they love to pray standing in the synagogues and on the corners of the streets, that they may be seen by men. Assuredly, I say to you, they have their reward. But you, when you pray, go into your room, and when you have shut your door, pray to your Father who is in the secret place; and your Father who sees in secret will reward you openly. And when you pray, do not use vain repetitions as the heathen do. For they think that they will be heard for their many words. "Therefore do not be like them. For your Father knows the things you have need of before you ask Him.

In this manner, therefore, pray:

Our Father in heaven,
Hallowed be Your name.
Your kingdom come.
Your will be done
On earth as it is in heaven.
Give us this day our daily bread.
And forgive us our debts,
As we forgive our debtors.
And do not lead us into temptation,
But deliver us from the evil one.
For Yours is the kingdom and
the power and the glory forever.
Amen.

HOW DID CHRIST PRAY?

Matt. 4:2 He fasted and prayed 40 days in the wilderness Mark 1:35 Now in the morning, having risen a long while before daylight, He went out and departed to a solitary place; and there He prayed.

Lk 6:12 He went out to a mountain and continued all night in prayer.

Matt. 26:39 In Gethsemane He fell on His face and prayed...not as I will, but as You will."

- He prayed in private. He prayer in public. He prayed on the cross. He prayed for his friends. He prayed for his enemies.

John 17:20 (*He prayed for us all.*) "I do not pray for these alone, but also for those who will believe in Me through their word;"

Heb 7:25 (*He still prays for us*) Therefore He is also able to save to the uttermost those who come to God through Him, since He always lives to make intercession for them.

- "Brethren, have you learned to pray?"
- Christ taught us to pray!

4. PRAYER CHANGES THINGS

- Mainly us!

1 Sam 1:27 (Hannah) For this child I prayed, and the Lord has granted me my petition which I asked of Him.

1 Chron 7:14 If My people who are called by My name will humble themselves, and pray and seek My face, and turn from their wicked ways, then I will hear from heaven, and will forgive their sin and heal their land.

Matt 7:7-8 Ask, and it will be given to you; seek, and you will find; knock, and it will be opened to you. For everyone who asks receives, and he who seeks finds, and to him who knocks it will be opened.

James 5:16 Confess your trespasses to one another, and pray for one another, that you may be healed. The effective, fervent prayer of a righteous man avails much.

<u>1 John 5:14-15</u> Now this is the confidence that we have in Him, that if we ask anything according to His will, He hears us. And if we know that He hears us, whatever we ask, we know that we have the petitions that we have asked of Him.

- Because we prayed, prayer changed things.

- Because we didn't pray, things didn't change.

LORD, WHAT A CHANGE!

Lord, what a change within us one short hour Spent in Thy Presence will prevail to make! What heavy burdens from our bosoms take!

What parched grounds refresh as with a shower!

We kneel and all around us seems to lower, We rise, and all, the distant and the near, Stands forth in sunny outline, bright and clear.

We kneel how weak, we rise how full of power! Why therefore should we do ourselves this wrong, Or others, that we are not always strong,

That we are ever overborne with care, That we should ever weak or heartless be, Anxious or troubled, when with us is prayer,

And joy and strength and courage are with Thee.

—*Trench* (KMB – pp.484-485)

- **Prayer changes things!**

CONCLUSION

<u>Luke 18:1</u> Then He spoke a parable to them, that men always ought to pray and not lose heart

1. Do you know that we ought always to pray?

2. Do you know that we ought never to lose heart?

3. Do you know that Christ taught us to pray?

4. Do you know that prayer changes things?

JUDSON ON PRAYER

Adoniram Judson, perhaps (one of) the greatest (missionaries) ever sent out from American shores, was emphatic in his insistence upon prayer. (He said) "Be resolute in prayer. Make any sacrifice to maintain it. Consider that time is short and that business and company must not be allowed to rob thee of thy business and company must not be allowed to rob thee of thy God." That was the man who impressed a mighty empire for God. (KMB–p.487)

WORK MORE ON YOUR KNEES

A preacher, while watching a marble cutter at work, exclaimed: "I wish I could deal such clanging blows on stony hearts!"

The workman replied: "Maybe you could if you worked like me, on your knees." (KMB–p.489)

Luke 18:1 Then He spoke a parable to them, that men always ought to pray and not lose heart,

- A person who claims to be a Christian but does not follow the example of Christ and keep His commandments is deceiving himself. (Daily Bible – p.523)

He who has My commandments and keeps them, it is
he who loves Me. And he who loves Me will be loved by
My Father, and I will love him and manifest
Myself to him. *John 14:21*

THE COMMANDS OF CHRIST #11

Have Faith In God

*Mark 11:22 So Jesus answered and said to them,
"Have faith in God."*

- Have faith in God.

1. TO HEAR YOUR PRAYERS

Ps 34:4 I sought the Lord, and He heard me, And delivered me from all my fears.

Prov 15:29 The Lord is far from the wicked, But He hears the prayer of the righteous.

Isa 59:1-2 Behold, the Lord's hand is not shortened, That it cannot save; Nor His ear heavy, That it cannot hear. But your iniquities have separated you from your God; And your sins have hidden His face from you, So that He will not hear.

<u>John 9:31</u> (*The man born blind whom Jesus healed*) Now we know that God does not hear sinners; but if anyone is a worshiper of God and does His will, He hears him.

<u>1 John 5:14-15</u> Now this is the confidence that we have in Him, that if we ask anything according to His will, He hears us. And if we know that He hears us, whatever we ask, we know that we have the petitions that we have asked of Him.

- Our heavenly Father hears every prayer that's prayed in His will in Jesus' name.

- Have faith in God to hear your prayers!

- Have faith in God.

2. TO ANSWER YOUR PRAYERS

<u>Matt 7:7-8</u> Ask, and it will be given to you; seek, and you will find; knock, and it will be opened to you. 8 For everyone who asks receives, and he who seeks finds, and to him who knocks it will be opened.

<u>John 15:7</u> If you abide in Me, and My words abide in you, you will ask what you desire, and it shall be done for you.

<u>James 5:16-18</u> Confess your trespasses to one another, and pray for one another, that you may be healed. The effective, fervent prayer of a righteous man avails much. *Elijah* was a man with a nature like ours, and he prayed earnestly that it would not rain;

and it did not rain on the land for three years and six months. 18 And he prayed again, and the heaven gave rain, and the earth produced its fruit.

HE NEVER DISAPPOINTS

"You seem in unusual pain today," I said one afternoon to a lady who suffered terribly and was also blind. Her response amazed me. "I once heard Pastor…preach, sir. It was in the days when I could see. He told us in his sermon of a visit to a friend who was dying, and when he asked him how he was, the answer came: 'My head is resting very sweetly on three pillows – infinite power, infinite love, and infinite wisdom! And my poor head is on those same pillows now, so that my heart is at rest. I go to God for comfort, and He never disappoints me." (KMB – pp.191-192)

• Have faith in God to answer your prayers!

• Have faith in God.

3. DO NOT DOUBT

• Why is the command to have faith in God so important?
  • So many do not!
  • Many struggle with their faith.
  • Many believe in false Gods.
  • Many believe in false religions.
  • Many believe only in self or what they can see or feel.

- You've got to have faith if you're going to be saved!

- You've got to have faith if you're going to stay saved!

- You've got to have faith if you're going to make it to heaven!

  - We're saved by faith!

  - We're sanctified by faith!

  - We're healed by faith!

Vvs.22-23 So Jesus answered and said to them, "Have faith in God. For assuredly, I say to you, whoever says to this mountain, 'Be removed and be cast into the sea,' and does not doubt in his heart, but believes that those things he says will be done, he will have whatever he says. Therefore I say to you, whatever things you ask when you pray, believe that you receive them, and you will have them."

John 20:27 Then He said to Thomas, "Reach your finger here, and look at My hands; and reach your hand here, and put it into My side. Do not be unbelieving, but believing."

1 Tim 2:8 I desire therefore that the men pray everywhere, lifting up holy hands, without wrath and doubting.

Heb 11:6 But without faith it is impossible to please Him, for he who comes to God must believe that He is, and that He is a rewarder of those who diligently seek Him.

James 1:5-8 If any of you lacks wisdom, let him ask of God, who gives to all liberally and without reproach, and it will be given to him. But let him ask in faith, with no doubting, for he who doubts is like a wave of the sea driven and tossed by the wind. For let not that man suppose that he will receive anything from the Lord; he is a double-minded man, unstable in all his ways.

THE ANTIDOTE FOR DOUBT

Faith in the Word of promise is the antidote for (doubt). Many a saint has stayed afloat amid the floods of mortal ills on (the words) "I am with thee." *Hudson Taylor,* sleeping on the temple steps outside inland cities in China with bandits feeling for his throat which they intended to cut, was kept in perfect peace by promises of God's presence. Faith bolstered up with the prop of promises cannot fail. (KMB – pp.192-193)

HOW TO KEEP FAITH BRIGHT

A woman who was showing a massive piece of family silver apologized as she took it from the cupboard. "Dreadfully tarnished!" she said, "I can't keep it bright unless I use it."

That is just as true of faith as it is of silver. Tucked away in the Sunday closet of the soul, and only brought out for show, it needs apology. You can't keep faith bright unless you use it. (KMB – p.193)

• Have faith in God. Do not doubt!

- Have faith in God.

4. KEEP IT SIMPLE STUPID

- The *kiss* method – the minister's wife who blew him kisses while he preached to remind him to Keep It Simple Stupid!

<u>Vvs.20-22</u> Now in the morning, as they passed by, they saw the fig tree dried up from the roots. And Peter, remembering, said to Him, "Rabbi, look! The fig tree which You cursed has withered away." So Jesus answered and said to them, "Have faith in God."

- God is trustworthy!
- No need to complicate faith.
- You either have faith or you do not have it.

<u>Matt 18:1-5</u>…The Bible teaches us to have faith as a little child:

Simple. Uncomplicated. Real

<u>Ps 37:5</u> Commit your way to the Lord, Trust also in Him, And He shall bring it to pass.

<u>Rom 8:28</u> And we know that all things work together for good to those who love God, to those who are the called according to His purpose.

<u>Rom 10:17</u> So then faith comes by hearing, and hearing by the word of God.

HOW MUCH HAVE YOU?
A friend tells of overhearing two little girls, playmates, who

were counting over their pennies. One said, "I have five pennies." The other said, "I have ten."

"No," said the first little girl, "you have just five cents, the same as I."

"But," the second child quickly replied, "my father said that when he came home tonight, he would give me five cents, and so I have ten cents."

The child's faith gave her proof of that which she did not as yet see, and she counted it as being already hers, because it had been already promised by her father. (KMB – p.194)

2 Cor 11:3 But I fear, lest somehow, as the serpent deceived Eve by his craftiness, so your minds may be corrupted from the simplicity that is in Christ.

- Have faith in God - Keep it simple stupid!

CONCLUSION

Mark 11:22 So Jesus answered and said to them, "Have faith in God."

1. Have faith in God…

2. To hear your prayers

3. To answer your prayers

4. Do not doubt

5. Keep it simple stupid

- How much faith does it take?

Matt 17:20 So Jesus said to them, "…assuredly, I say to you, if you have faith as a mustard seed, you will say to this mountain, 'Move from here to there,' and it will move; and nothing will be impossible for you."

LEARNING

You will never learn faith in comfortable surroundings. God gives us the promises in a quiet hour; God seals our covenants with great and gracious words, then He steps back and waits to see how much we believe; then He lets the tempter come, and the test seems to contradict all that He has spoken. *It is then that faith wins its crown.* That is the time to look up through the storm, and among the trembling, frightened seamen cry, "I believe God, that it shall be even as it was told me. - By Mrs. Charles E. Cowman (KMB – p.192)

- Have faith in God!
- Have faith in God's word!

John 14:15 If you love Me, keep My commandments.

Rev 22:14 Blessed are those who do His commandments, that they may have the right to the tree of life, and may enter through the gates into the city.

If you keep My commandments, you will abide in
My love, just as I have kept My Father's commandments
and abide in His love. *John 15:10*

THE COMMANDS OF CHRIST #12

You Should Do As I Have Done To You

PRACTICE THE ORDINANCES
Baptism, Feetwashing and Communion

*<u>John 13:15</u> For I have given you an example,
that you should do as I have done to you.*

- Dr. Lawrence Chesnut once brought a message on "The Importance of the Ordinances."
- In that message, he shared concerning why we do what we do. He said that there are three phases of Christ's redemptive work:
  1. His humiliation (coming to earth, suffering)
  2. His death
  3. His resurrection
- Likewise, we in the church of God believe that there are

three corresponding ordinances that portray the three phaes of Christ's redemptive work.;

1. His humiliation - Feetwashing
2. His death - The Lord's Supper/Communion
3. His resurrection - Baptism

- In the Old Testament, the Jews had three feasts that all male Jews were required to attend each year:

1. Passover
2. Pentecost
3. Tabernacles

- An ordinance is "an outward symbol divinely appointed to represent a great fact or truth of the gospel and the personal relation of the recipient to that fact or truth." (Byrum, p.556)

- We use the term "ordinance" rather than sacrament because other groups have emphasized the belief that a sacrament bestows grace upon the recipient and is neces sary for salvation. Some church groups, however, use the word sacrament with no idea of merit. (There are non-ordinance groups, too.)

- "If we call these symbols 'ordinances' I think we shall be better able to get away from the superstitions of long, moldy ages of ignorance. Since they were ordained by Christ, why not call them ordinances?" (C.E. Brown)

- As there are three ordinances to consider, let us begin where most Christians must begin after being saved, baptism.

1. BAPTISM (HIS RESURRECTION)

V.19 Go therefore and make disciples of all the nations, baptizing them in the name of the Father and of the Son and of the Holy Spirit,

Key Verse 20…Teaching them to observe all things that I have commanded you;

- Here we have Christ's command to baptize.

EIGHT THINGS ABOUT BAPTISM

1. It is for believers only!

2. It does not cleanse us from sin. It is symbolic of that cleansing, but only the blood of Jesus can wash away our sins.

3. It is an outward witness of an inner experience.

4. It is by immersion. It symbolizes a death and a burial. (Rom 6)

5. It testifies to our belief in the resurrection of the Lord.

6. It symbolizes a personal resurrection from a life of sin to a new life in Christ.

7. It says we believe there will be a resurrection when Jesus comes again.

8. It is "the answer of a good conscience toward God" (1 Pet. 3:21)

Acts 24:16 (*Paul told Felix the Governor*) "This being so, I myself always strive to have a conscience without offense toward God and men."

<u>Acts 8:35-39</u> Then Philip opened his mouth, and beginning at this Scripture, preached Jesus to him. Now as they went down the road, they came to some water. And the eunuch said, "See, here is water. What hinders me from being baptized?" Then Philip said, "If you believe with all your heart, you may." And he answered and said, "I believe that Jesus Christ is the Son of God." So he commanded the chariot to stand still. And both Philip and the eunuch went down into the water, and he baptized him. Now when they came up out of the water, the Spirit of the Lord caught Philip away, so that the eunuch saw him no more; and he went on his way rejoicing.

<u>Acts 16:30-34</u> And he brought them out and said, "Sirs, what must I do to be saved?" So they said, "Believe on the Lord Jesus Christ, and you will be saved, you and your household." Then they spoke the word of the Lord to him and to all who were in his house. And he took them the same hour of the night and washed their stripes. And immediately he and all his family were baptized. Now when he had brought them into his house, he set food before them; and he rejoiced, having believed in God with all his household.

All believers see baptism as a rite of identification with the Lord Jesus. It should be a unifying factor, for in every baptism there is a statement of relationship to the risen Lord. (QT – 3.12.99)

2. FEETWASHING (HIS HUMILIATION)

- Most church groups accept two New Testament ordinances: Baptism and the Lord's Supper (Communion). But, we in the Church of God, along with some others, accept a third ordinance, that of Feetwashing.

- To meet the criteria of an ordinance, four things must be met. We shall show that feetwashing, just like baptism and communion meets these four criteria:

1. An ordinance must be instituted by divine authority.
- There can be no doubt that Jesus instituted the practice of feetwashing.

V.15...For I have given you an example, that you should do as I have done to you.

2. It had to be an outward act practiced by Christ.
- Again, we have abundant proof of this.
  Jn 13:5...He began to wash the disciples' feet.

3. It must be divinely commanded to be practiced by all Christians perpetually.

Vv.14-15 If I then, your Lord and Teacher, have washed your feet, you also ought to wash one another's feet. For I have given you an example, that you should do as I have done to you.

- What Jesus commanded the first disciples to observe is commanded to *all* Christians, for He told them to "Go therefore and make disciples of all the nations...teaching them to observe all things that I have commanded you.

(Key Verse 20)

In the movie, *Bridge over the River Kwai*, the commanding officer in the Japanese prison camp makes a suggestion about not trying to escape. One of the men is discussing this suggestion with a fellow prisoner, and he said, "Since he only 'suggested' it, we can do as we please." The fellow prisoner said to him, "Listen, when a man of his position 'suggests' something, it's an order."

- When Christ said, "you ought." THAT WAS A COMMAND!

4. **It must represent an important religious truth and the Christian's relation to it.**
- Feetwashing symbolizes humility, service, and unity.

IT TEACHES HUMILITY

Luke 22:24 Now there was also a dispute among them, as to which of them should be considered the greatest.

- This spirit most likely occasioned the institution of this ordinance. And, this wasn't the only time the disciples demonstrated such a spirit.

IT TEACHES OUR POSITION IN THE CHURCH

Matt 23:8 "But you, do not be called "Rabbi"; for One is your Teacher, the Christ, and you are all brethren.

- "In the church of God there are no big I's and little you's. In this humble ordinance we show our place among the brethren – at their feet." (H.M. Riggle)

IT TEACHES THAT WE ARE SERVANTS

- Jesus too the place of a servant...so should we!

IT TEACHES THAT WE HONOR CHRIST

<u>Matt 25:40</u> "Assuredly, I say to you, inasmuch as you did it to one of the least of these My brethren, you did it to Me."

- (H.M. Riggle) "Every time we wash our brethren's feet, we wash Jesus' feet."

- Feetwashing is a Bible ordinance because it meets all the criteria needed:
  1. Christ taught it.
  2. Christ practiced it.
  3. Christ commanded its observance for all time.
  4 It represents an important religious truth and the Christian's relation to it.

- All three ordinances are needed to portray all the relation-ships of the Christian. If any ordinance is omitted, the picture is incomplete.

  1. Baptism–the Christian to the world (dead)
  2. Feetwashing–the Christian to other Christians (servants–on the same level)
  3. Communion–the Christian to the Lord Jesus (partakers of His body & blood)

"AND BE BAPTIZED"

Jesus said, "He that would be great, let him become the servant of all." Foot washing is the symbol of service, the badge of the humble servant. We must never forget that our Lord took a towel and conquered the world. The inspired writer reminds us that we should "in honor, prefer one another." And Christ gives the injunction, "If I then, your Lord and Master, have washed our feet; ye also ought to wash one another's feet. For I have given you an example, that ye should do as I have done to you" (John 13:15). Humility is so characteristic of the Christian spirit that we ought regularly, systematically, and graphically to keep reminding ourselves "what manner of spirit we are of." Thousands of God's children find revealed strength in the observance of foot washing. (Hillery C. Rice – pp.22-24)

- The 74-year-old woman at Ruston, Louisiana, who asked if she could participate in our feetwashing service. She had always wanted to participate, but her church didn't observe feetwashing. She received a great blessing!

3. COMMUNION (HIS DEATH)

- "As the Passover of the Mosaic dispensation was predictive of the great truth of sacrificial atonement, so the Lord's Supper is commemorative of the same truth." (Byrum)

1. The broken bread and fruit of the vine poured forth are symbols of the atoning sufferings and death of Christ.

- Bread = His body. Bread of Life (unleavened, no sin, no hypocrisy, sincerity and truth)

- Fruit of the vine = unfermented grape juice; Christ's shed blood (also "cup of communion")

2. The eating of the bread and drinking of the fruit of the vine by the participant is symbolic of his personal trust in the atonement of Christ, for his individual salvation and for the sustaining of his spiritual life.

3. I agree with Byrum and others who teach that "those should not participate in the communion supper who have not been converted (saved), or who have backslidden and openly lived a disorderly life (of sin).'

1 Cor 11:27-28 Therefore whoever eats this bread or drinks this cup of the Lord in an unworthy manner will be guilty of the body and blood of the Lord. But let a man examine himself, and so let him eat of the bread and drink of the cup.

- As we teach that baptism is for believers, so we teach that the Lord's supper and feetwashing are also for believers.

4. The Lord's Supper is commemorative of the death of Christ.

1 Cor 11:23-26 For I received from the Lord that which I also delivered to you: that the Lord Jesus on the same night in which He was betrayed took bread; 24 and when He had given thanks, He broke it and said, "Take, eat; this is My body which is broken for you; do this in remembrance of Me." 25 In the same manner He also took the cup after supper, saying, "This cup is the

new covenant in My blood. This do, as often as you drink it, in remembrance of Me." 26 For as often as you eat this bread and drink this cup, you proclaim the Lord's death till He comes.

- "The worldly man drinks to forget. The Christian drinks to remember."

- Before we go to the table to eat, we make sure we have clean hands.

- (ODB–10.1.95) "Before you come to the Lord's table, make sure you have a clean heart."

5.   The Lord's Supper is representative of the unity of Christians in one body, the church.

- One loaf = one body of believers in Christ

1 Cor 12:12, 18, 20, 27 Many members – one body

1 Cor 10:16-17 The cup of blessing which we bless, is it not the communion of the blood of Christ? The bread which we break, is it not the communion of the body of Christ? For we, though many, are one bread and one body; for we all partake of that one bread.

Eph 3:14-15 For this reason I bow my knees to the Father of our Lord Jesus Christ, from whom the whole family in heaven and earth is named.

CONCLUSION

<u>John 13:15</u> For I have given you an example, that you should do as I have done to you.

"Constantly enlarge the area of your conversion. Make your conversion take in more and more areas of your life. In India we gave the servants, including the sweeper, a holiday one day each week, and we volunteered to do their jobs for them. The sweepers' work included the cleaning of the latrines before the days of flush toilets. No one would touch that job but an outcast, but we volunteered. One day I said to a Brahmin convert who was hesitating to volunteer; Brother when are you going to volunteer?" He shook his head slowly and said, "Brother Stanley, I'm converted, but I'm not converted that far." Some of our conversions are "Conversions, Limited.' Some are 'Conversions, Unlimited. How converted are you? *(E. Stanley Jones)*

1. Have you been baptized? (Remembering His Resurrection)

2. Have you participated in feetwashing? (Remembering His Humiliation)

3. Have you taken communion? (Remembering His Death)

- None of these will save you in themselves, but obedience to "Christ's Commands" are important after we've been saved.

- Under most circumstances, most Christians are able to comply with the requirements of each ordinance.

<u>Luke 6:46 </u>But why do you call Me "Lord, Lord," and not do the things which I say?

<u>James 1:22 </u>But be doers of the word, and not hearers only, deceiving yourselves.

You are My friends if you do whatever
I command you. *John 15:14*

THE COMMANDS OF CHRIST #13

Whatever You Want Men To Do To You, Do Also To Them

Matthew 7:12 *Therefore, whatever you want men to do to you, do also to them, for this is the Law and the Prophets.*

1. THE GOLDEN RULE

- This verse is commonly known as the Golden Rule.

- It's part of the Sermon on the Mount (Matt 5-7).

- Why is this called the Golden Rule?

- Because it was highly honored by the Lord, and because gold represents the most precious metal on earth.

- Many advocate doing unto others *before* they do unto you.

- Others say The Golden Rule means, "Them that has the gold rules."

- Dr. Adam Clarke renders this verse such: "Guided by justice and mercy, do unto all men as you would have them do to you, were your circumstances and theirs reversed."

The so-called golden rule (12) summarizes the law and the prophets; that is, the Old Testament. *Christianity is not anything less, but it is something more.*

The golden rule had been stated in negative form before Christ appeared. Confucius said: "Do not unto others what you would not have them do unto you." The Jewish rabbis had a similar saying. *But it is generally recognized that Jesus was the first to give it a positive form.* This is something far different. To refrain from hurting is one thing; to lend a helping hand is another. (Beacon)

Lev 19:18 You shall not take vengeance, nor bear any grudge against the children of your people, but you shall love your neighbor as yourself: I am the Lord.

Obad 1:15 For the day of the Lord upon all the nations is near; As you have done, it shall be done to you; Your reprisal shall return upon your own head.

Luke 6:38 Give, and it will be given to you: good measure, pressed down, shaken together, and running over will be put into your bosom. For with the same measure that you use, it will be measured back to you.

Gal 5:14 For all the law is fulfilled in one word, even in this: "You shall love your neighbor as yourself."

1 Thess 5:15 See that no one renders evil for evil to anyone, but always pursue what is good both for yourselves and for all.

The Golden Rule is precious in the sight of God and to those who keep it!

2. THE ROYAL LAW

<u>Jas 2:8</u> If you really fulfill the royal law according to the Scripture, "You shall love your neighbor as yourself," you do well.

In this [verse] James brings us back to a basic rule for the Christian—Thou shalt love thy neighbor as thyself We shall always do well if we always do as we would like others to do to us if conditions were reversed. (Beacon)

This law for the guidance of Christian conduct is according to the scripture. It is quoted from the Old Testament (Lev. 19:18) and reaffirmed in the teachings of Jesus (Matt. 22:39). It is the royal law because it is the word of our Lord; it is the royal law because when it is kept in deed and in truth we cannot break any of God's laws governing our relationships with our fellowman. The keeping of this law is the keeping of all.

- Notice the truth in principle that Jesus taught is referred to in high sounding language – i.e. golden rule; royal law.

- It is a wise and good thing to keep the golden rule/ royal law..

<u>Matt 20:25-28</u> But Jesus called them to Himself and said, "You know that the rulers of the Gentiles lord it over them, and those who are great exercise authority over them. Yet it shall not be so

among you; but whoever desires to become great among you, let him be your servant. And whoever desires to be first among you, let him be your slave—just as the Son of Man did not come to be served, but to serve, and to give His life a ransom for many.

- **Those who keep the royal law seek to serve, not rule!**

<u>Rom 8:16-17</u> The Spirit Himself bears witness with our spirit that we are children of God, and if children, then heirs— heirs of God and joint heirs with Christ, if indeed we suffer with Him, that we may also be glorified together.

- **If we are children of God, we will strive to keep the royal law!**

3. DO AS JESUS DID

- WWJD = What Would Jesus Do?

<u>1 Peter 2:21</u> For to this you were called, because Christ also suffered for us, leaving us an example, that you should follow His steps.

- "In His Steps"–Sheldon

- HCWKWJWDIWDKWHD = How Can We Know What Jesus Would Do If We Don't Know What He Did?

Matthew 5:43-48

You have heard that it was said, "You shall love your neighbor and hate your enemy." But I say to you, love your enemies, bless those who curse you, do good to those who hate you, and pray for those who spitefully use you and persecute you, that you may be sons of your Father in heaven; for He makes His sun rise on the evil and on the good, and sends rain on the just and on the unjust. For if you love those who love you, what reward have you? Do not even the tax collectors do the same? And if you greet your brethren only, what do you do more than others? Do not even the tax collectors do so? Therefore you shall be perfect, just as your Father in heaven is perfect.

- Actions

- Reactions

Acts 10:38 how God anointed Jesus of Nazareth with the Holy Spirit and with power, who went about doing good and healing all who were oppressed by the devil, for God was with Him.

Rom 12:17-21 Repay no one evil for evil. Have regard for good things in the sight of all men. If it is possible, as much as depends on you, live peaceably with all men. Beloved, do not avenge yourselves, but rather give place to wrath; for it is written, "Vengeance is Mine, I will repay," says the Lord. Therefore

If your enemy is hungry, feed him;
If he is thirsty, give him a drink;

For in so doing you will heap coals of fire on his head. Do not be overcome by evil, but overcome evil with good. Gal 6:7-10 Do not be deceived, God is not mocked; for whatever a man sows, that he will also reap. For he who sows to his flesh will of the flesh reap corruption, but he who sows to the Spirit will of the Spirit reap everlasting life. And let us not grow weary while doing good, for in due season we shall reap if we do not lose heart. Therefore, as we have opportunity, let us do good to all, especially to those who are of the household of faith.

- Paul had a good spirit in spite of his afflictions and prison life.

- Paul had much to say about relational living.

- The way we are treated is sometimes a reflection of how we treat others. Not so with Paul.

- If you're being purposely mistreated/abused, perhaps you can reverse the treatment by treating your enemy nice in spite of their abuse.

- Everything Jesus did was for the good of others and for the glory of God.

- If we do as Jesus did we'll always keep the golden rule!

4. DUE UNTO OTHERS

<u>Rom 13:8-10</u> Owe no one anything except to love one another, for he who loves another has fulfilled the law. For the commandments, "You shall not commit adultery," "You shall not murder," "You shall not steal," "You shall not bear false witness," "You shall not covet," and if there is any other commandment, are all summed up in this saying, namely, "You shall love your neighbor as yourself." Love does no harm to a neighbor; therefore love is the fulfillment of the law.

- What is due others?

  - Loving our neighbors as ourselves.

  - Right treatment.

  - Christlike love.

  - Keeping the Golden Rule.

  - Practicing the Royal Law.

  - Our Christianity is relational, not only to God, but especially to humanity.

1 Cor 13:4-8 Love is patient, love is kind. It does not envy, it does not boast, it is not proud. It is not rude, it is not self- seeking, it is not easily angered, it keeps no record of wrongs. Love does not delight in evil but rejoices with the truth. It always protects, always trusts, always hopes, always perseveres. Love never fails...

Luke 10:25-37 The Good Samaritan

And behold, a certain lawyer stood up and tested Him, saying, "Teacher, what shall I do to inherit eternal life?" He said to him, "What is written in the law? What is your reading of it?" So he answered and said, "'You shall love the Lord your God with all your heart, with all your soul, with all your strength, and with all your mind,' and 'your neighbor as yourself.'" And He said to him, "You have answered rightly; do this and you will live." But he, wanting to justify himself, said to Jesus, "And who is my neighbor?" Then Jesus answered and said: "A certain man went down from Jerusalem to Jericho, and fell among thieves, who stripped him of his clothing, wounded him, and departed, leaving him half dead. Now by chance a certain priest came down that road. And when he saw him, he passed by on the other side. Likewise a Levite, when he arrived at the place, came and looked, and passed by on the other side. But a certain Samaritan, as he journeyed, came where he was. And when he saw him, he had compassion. So he went to him and bandaged his wounds, pouring on oil and wine; and he set him on his own animal, brought him to an inn, and took care of him. On the next day, when he departed, he took out two denarii, gave them to the innkeeper, and said to him, 'Take care of him; and whatever more you spend, when I come again, I will repay you.' *So which of these three do you think was neighbor to him who fell among the thieves?"* And he said, "He who showed mercy on him." Then Jesus said to him, "Go and do likewise."

1 John 4:20-21 If someone says, "I love God," and hates his brother, he is a liar; for he who does not love his brother whom he has seen, how can he love God whom he has not seen? 21 And this commandment we have from Him: that he who loves God must love his brother also.

- Let us be sure that we give others what is due them in the Lord, whether they deserve it not!

CONCLUSION

Matt 7:12 Therefore, whatever you want men to do to you, do also to them, for this is the Law and the Prophets.

1. Jesus commands us to keep the Golden Rule
2. James says we ought to practice the Royal Law

3. We should strive to do as Jesus did (and would have us do)

4. Let us remember what is due unto others

    - Loving our neighbors as ourselves

    - Right treatment

    - Christlike love

IS THE GOLDEN RULE TO BE OBEYED TODAY?

- Certainly! The Old Testament law of duty should be surpassed by the New Testament law of love!

- Many contend that rules are made to be broken, but Christ would teach us the significance of keeping His rules.

- "Never till our Lord came down this to teach did men effectually and widely exemplify it in their practice." (Brown)

- If you would not be hated, do not hate.

- If you would have friends, be friendly.

- If you despise vengeance, do not be vengeful.

- If you would not be cheated, don't be a cheater.

- If you dislike thievery, do not steal.

- If you would not be taken advantage of, do not take advantage of others.

- If you would be forgiven, you must be forgiving.

- If you would be loved, you must be loving!

- "None but he whose heart is filled with love to God and all mankind can keep this precept, either in its spirit or letter." (Clarke)

IF WE PRACTICED THE GOLDEN RULE:

- Our churches would run smoother.

- Our marriages would be happier and last longer.

- Our prisons would be empty.

- Our courts would be useless.

- Our world would be a better place.

- We would be better people.

- And Christ would be glorified in our lives.

- Are you keeping Christ's commandment to "do unto others as you would have them do unto you?"

- Blatant disobedience always leads to disaster in the spiritual realm.

Matthew 7:24-27

Therefore whoever hears these sayings of Mine, and does them, I will liken him to a wise man who built his house on the rock: and the rain descended, the floods came, and the winds blew and beat on that house; and it did not fall, for it was founded on the rock. "But everyone who hears these sayings of Mine, and does not do them, will be like a foolish man who built his house on the sand: and the rain descended, the floods came, and the winds blew and beat on that house; and it fell. And great was its fall."

- A person who claims to be a Christian but does not follow the example of Christ and keep His commandments is deceiving himself.

John 14:15 "If you love Me, keep My commandments."

Rev 22:14 Blessed are those who do His commandments, that they may have the right to the tree of life, and may enter through the gates into the city.

Finally then, brethren, we urge and exhort in the Lord
Jesus that you should abound more and more, just as you received from us how you ought to walk and to please God;
for you know what commandments we gave you through
the Lord Jesus. *1 Thessalonians 4:1-2*

THE COMMANDS OF CHRIST #14

Give, And It Will Be Given To You

Luke 6:38 Give, and it will be given to you: good measure, pressed down, shaken together, and running over will be put into your bosom. For with the same measure that you use, it will be measured back to you.

1. THE SIMPLE COMMAND
Luke 6:38 "Give."

OLD TESTAMENT

Ex 30:15 The rich shall not give more and the poor shall not give less. When you give an offering to the Lord, to make atonement for yourselves.

Deut 16:16-17 Three times a year all your males shall appear before the Lord your God in the place which He chooses: at the

Feast of Unleavened Bread, at the Feast of Weeks, and at the Feast of Tabernacles; and they shall not appear before the Lord empty-handed. Every man shall give as he is able, according to the blessing of the Lord your God which He has given you."

NEW TESTAMENT

- "Jesus often spoke on money matters' because money matters!"

Matt 23:23 Woe to you, scribes and Pharisees, hypocrites! For you pay tithe of mint and anise and cummin, and have neglected the weightier matters of the law: justice and mercy and faith. These you ought to have done, without leaving the others undone.

1 Cor 16:1-2 Now concerning the collection for the saints, as I have given orders to the churches of Galatia, so you must do also: On the first day of the week let each one of you lay something aside, storing up as he may prosper, that there be no collections when I come.

Luke 6:38 "Give."

- What am I commanded to give?
- Give yourself
- (Prov. 23:26 "My son, give me your heart...")
- Give your time
- Give your talent/ability
- Give your energy/strength
- Give your money (tithes and offerings. "10/5 Rule" = 10% tithe and 5% offerings)

- Jesus commands us to give not because He needs the money, but because we need to give for the glory of God, the good of others, and the good it will do us to give!

2. THE BLESSED PROMISE

Luke 6:38

Give, and it will be given to you: good measure, pressed down, shaken together, and running over will be put into your bosom.

- **How will He give?**
  - Generously
  - Abundantly
  - Willingly/Freely
  - He gives in what He sends
  - He gives in what He saves

Matt 7:7-8 Ask, and it will be given to you; seek, and you will find; knock, and it will be opened to you. For everyone who asks receives, and he who seeks finds, and to him who knocks it will be opened.

1 Cor 1:20 For all the promises of God in Him are Yes, and in Him Amen, to the glory of God through us.

Phil 4:19 And my God shall supply all your need according to His riches in glory by Christ Jesus.

<u>2 Peter 1:4</u> by which have been given to us exceedingly great and precious promises, that through these you may be partakers of the divine nature, having escaped the corruption that is in the world through lust.

- Why are we so quick to believe some promises and so slow to believe others?

STANDING ON THE PROMISES

Standing on the promises of Christ my King, Thro' eternal ages let His praises ring;

Glory in the highest, I will shout and sing, Standing on the promises of God.

4. THE DIVINE LAW

Luke 6:38

Give, and it will be given to you: good measure, pressed down, shaken together, and running over will be put into your bosom. For with the same measure that you use, it will be measured back to you."

- You have to give before you get.
- You have to sow before you reap.
- You have to die before you live.

<u>John 12:24</u> Most assuredly, I say to you, unless a grain of wheat falls into the ground and dies, it remains alone; but if it dies, it produces much grain.

- You have to make a deposit before you can make a withdrawal.

Matt 6:19-21 Do not lay up for yourselves treasures on earth, where moth and rust destroy and where thieves break in and steal; but lay up for yourselves treasures in heaven, where neither moth nor rust destroys and where thieves do not break in and steal. For where your treasure is, there your heart will be also.

- Many wish to put in the minimum and withdraw the maximum. But it doesn't work that way!

Malachi 3:8-12

"Will a man rob God? Yet you rob me. But you ask, 'How do we rob you?' In tithes and offerings. 9 You are under a curse —the whole nation of you—because you are robbing me. 10 Bring the whole tithe into the storehouse, that there may be food in my house. Test me in this," says the Lord Almighty, "and see if I will not throw open the floodgates of heaven and pour out so much blessing that you will not have room enough for it. I will prevent pests from devouring your crops, and the vines in your fields will not cast their fruit," says the Lord Almighty. "Then all the nations will call you blessed, for yours will be a delightful land," says the Lord Almighty. (NIV)

Acts 20:35 I have shown you in every way, by laboring like this, that you must support the weak. And remember the words of the Lord Jesus, that He said, "It is more blessed to give than to receive."

2 Cor 8:12 For if there is first a willing mind, it is accepted according to what one has, and not according to what he does not have.

GENEROUS

Teofilo said to Christobel the new convert in the little mission chapel in Cuba: "Christobel, if you had a hundred sheep, would you give fifty of them for the Lord's work?"

"Yes, I would."

"Would you do the same if you had a hundred cows?"

"Yes, Teofilo, I would."

"Would you do the same if you had a hundred horses?"

"Yes, of course."

"If you had two pigs, would you give one of them to Him?"

"No, I wouldn't; and you have no right to ask me, Teofilo, for you know I have two pigs." (KMB – p.239)

2 Cor 9:6-7 But this I say: He who sows sparingly will also reap sparingly, and he who sows bountifully will also reap bountifully. So let each one give as he purposes in his heart, not grudgingly or of necessity; for God loves a cheerful giver.

Gal 6:7-10 Do not be deceived, God is not mocked; for whatever a man sows, that he will also reap. For he who sows to his flesh will of the flesh reap corruption, but he who sows to the Spirit will of the Spirit reap everlasting life. And let us not grow weary while doing good, for in due season we shall reap if we do not lose heart. Therefore, as we have opportunity, let us do good to all, especially to those who are of the household of faith.

Mark 12:41-44 Remember "The Widow's Mite"

A LITTLE GIRL'S PENNIES

Hattie Wyatt, a little girl, came to a small Sunday school and asked to be taken in, but it was explained there was no room for her. In less than two years she fell ill, and slipped away on her own little last pilgrimage, and no one guessed her strange little secret until beneath her pillow was found a torn pocketbook with fifty-seven pennies in it, wrapped in a scrap of paper on which was written, "To help build the little Temple bigger, so that more children can go to Sunday School."

For two years she had saved her pennies for the cause which was nearest her heart. The pastor told the incident to his congregation, and the people began making donations for the enlargement. *The papers told it far and wide, and within five years those fifty-seven pennies had grown to be $250,000*, and today in Philadelphia, can be seen a great church, the Baptist Temple, seating 3,300, a Temple College with accommodations for more than 1,400 students, a Temple Hospital, and a Temple Sunday school so large that all who wish may come and be comfortable. She was only a little girl, but who can estimate the result of her unselfishness, and her fifty-seven pennies? (KMB – p.240)

CONCLUSION

<u>Luke 6:38</u> "Give, and it will be given to you: good measure, pressed down, shaken together, and running over will be put into your bosom. For with the same measure that you use, it will be measured back to you."

1. Have you obeyed *the simple command?*

2. Do you believe *the blessed promise?*

3. Have you proven *the divine law* to be true for yourself?

PLACING MONEY IN CHRIST'S HAND

A pastor was (receiving) a missionary (offering)…when he said, "I want each of you to give today as though you were putting your money right into the pierced hand of Jesus Christ."

A lady came up afterward, and said, "I was going to give a half-dollar, but I did not do so."

"Why did you not do it?" the preacher asked.

"Do you think I would put a half-dollar into his pierced hand? I have ten dollars at home, and I am going to give that." (KMB – p.246)

- If we were putting our money into the pierced hand of our Lord our contributions would amount to millions, and the world would be evangelized in ten years.

- Let's get busy and give as unto the Lord—into his nail-pierced hands!

- A church cannot do without workers and givers.

- A person who claims to be a Christian but does not follow the example of Christ and keep His commandments is deceiving himself.

John 14:15 "If you love Me, keep My commandments."

Rev 22:14 Blessed are those who do His commandments, that they may have the right to the tree of life, and may enter through the gates into the city.

But be doers of the word, and not hearers only,
deceiving yourselves. *James 1:22*

THE COMMANDS OF CHRIST #15

And You Shall Be Witness To Me

Acts 1:8 But you shall receive power when the Holy Spirit
\has come upon you; and you shall be witnesses to Me in Jerusalem,
and in all Judea and Samaria, and to the end of the earth."

1. YOU SHALL RECEIVE POWER

<u>Acts 1:4</u> And being assembled together with them, He commanded them not to depart from Jerusalem, but to wait for the Promise of the Father, "which," He said, "you have heard from Me.

The disciples were not yet adequately equipped for their major offensive against the enemy. So their General issued the order that they were to wait (lit. "remain around") until empowered by the Holy Spirit for carrying out their commission.

This strong emphasis on the baptism with the Holy Spirit, as being greater and more essential than the baptism with water, anticipates the central thrust of the Book of Acts. Any Christianity that neglects the Spirit-baptism is incomplete and pre-Pentecost. Without this baptism there would have been no Book of Acts, and in fact no Church of Jesus Christ today. Without the baptism of the Holy Spirit in personal experience there is no adequate enablement for victorious living and effective service. (Beacon)

Luke 24:49

Behold, I send the Promise of My Father upon you; but tarry in the city of Jerusalem until you are   endued with power from on high.

Key Verse 8…But you shall receive power when the Holy Spirit has come upon you; and you shall be witnesses to Me in Jerusalem, and in all Judea and Samaria, and to the end of the earth.

- Not might, but shall.
- Dr. O.L. Johnson said the Holy Spirit gives us…
  1. The power to be
  2. The power to see
  3. The power to say
  4. The power to stay

POWER

1. <u>Exousia</u> (v. 7). = "authority" The Greek word properly means: "freedom to exercise the inward force or faculty expressed by *dynamis*," and so "right" or "authority."

2. Dynamis (v8) = implies "the possession of the ability to make power felt," whereas *exousia* "affirms that free movement is ensured to the ability." (Beacon)

- You shall receive sanctifying, Holy Spirit power.

- You shall receive enabling power.

- Moral power

- Spiritual power

John 16:7-14

Nevertheless I tell you the truth. It is to your advantage that I go away; for if I do not go away, the Helper will not come to you; but if I depart, I will send Him to you. And when He has come, *He will convict the world of sin, and of righteousness, and of judgment*: of sin, because they do not believe in Me; of righteousness, because I go to My Father and you see Me no more; of judgment, because the ruler of this world is judged. "I still have many things to say to you, but you cannot bear them now. However, when He, the Spirit of truth, has come, *He will guide you into all truth*; for He will not speak on His own authority, but whatever He hears He will speak; and He will tell you things to come. *He will glorify Me*, for He will take of what is Mine and declare it to you.

Dan 11:32 But the people who know their God shall be strong, and carry out great exploits.

2 Tim 1:7 For God has not given us a spirit of fear, but of power and of love and of a sound mind.

- **His Power Is Adequate–The Rolls Royce Story**

A man was thinking of buying a new Rolls Royce. He asked the salesman about the horsepower. The salesman told him that he would have to write the manufacturer in England to find out. A few days later he called the customer and told him the manufacturer had written back and given him an answer. He said the horsepower was "Adequate." (*So is the power of the Holy Spirit*)

2 Tim 2:21 Therefore if anyone cleanses himself from the latter, he will be a vessel for honor, sanctified and useful for the Master, prepared for every good work.

Key Verse 8... "But you shall receive power when the Holy Spirit has come upon you; and you shall be witnesses to Me in Jerusalem, and in all Judea and Samaria, and to the end of the earth."

- **And they did!**

  - Peter did

  - John did

  - Stephen did

  - Paul did

  - Evangelist Earl Moore did

  - Corrie ten Boom did

  - I did!

Acts 2:1-4 (*And you can, too!*) When the Day of Pentecost had fully come, they were all with one accord in one place. And suddenly there came a sound from heaven, as of a rushing mighty wind, and it filled the whole house where they were sitting. Then there appeared to them divided tongues, as of fire, and one sat upon each of them. And they were all filled with the Holy Spirit and began to speak with other tongues, as the Spirit gave them utterance.

The significance of these two symbols–wind and fire–is too obvious to miss. Wind (2) and fire (3) were an accepted symbolism for the powerful and cleansing operation of God's Spirit." *That is, when the Holy Spirit fills the believer's heart He gives both power and purity.* No person can have one without the other. To receive the Holy Spirit in His fullness is to experience both simultaneously. (Beacon)

2. YOU SHALL BE WITNESSES

Key Verse 8...But you shall receive power when the Holy Spirit has come upon you; and you shall be witnesses to Me in Jerusalem, and in all Judea and Samaria, and to the end of the earth.

Acts 1:8 is the key verse of this significant book. It gives at once both the power and the program of the Church...The power is the Holy Spirit. The program is the evangelization of the world. *For a person to claim to be filled with the Spirit and yet not to be vitally concerned about world missions is to deny his profession.* When the Holy Spirit fills the human heart with His power and presence, He generates the urge to carry out Christ's command. The converse is also true: *the Great Commission cannot be fulfilled without the power of the Spirit.*

This verse also indicates the three main divisions of the Book of Acts: (1) Witnessing in Jerusalem (chapters 1-7); Witnessing in all Judea and Samaria (chapters 8-12); (3) Witnessing in the Gentile World (chapters 13-28). (Beacon)

Key Verse 8…and you shall be witnesses…

- Not judges
- Not prosecuting attorneys
- But witnesses

Matt 5:16 Let your light so shine before men, that they may see your good works and glorify your Father in heaven.

Matt 10:32-33 Therefore whoever confesses Me before men, him I will also confess before My Father who is in heaven. 3But whoever denies Me before men, him I will also deny before My Father who is in heaven."

Acts 4:31,33 And when they had prayed, the place where they were assembled together was shaken; and they were all filled with the Holy Spirit, and they spoke the word of God with boldness. And with great power the apostles gave witness to the resurrection of the Lord Jesus. And great grace was upon them all.

Peter 3:15 But sanctify the Lord God in your hearts, and always be ready to give a defense to everyone who asks you a reason for the hope that is in you, with meekness and fear.

Peter 1:16 For we did not follow cunningly devised fables when we made known to you the power and coming of our Lord Jesus Christ, but were eyewitnesses of His majesty.

Key Verse 8…and you shall be witnesses to Me.

- Before Kings

- Before political leaders
- Before religious leaders
- Before the common folk
- Before unbelievers

Key Verse 8…and you shall be witnesses to Me.

- **And they were!**

Acts 8:1,4 Now Saul was consenting to his death. At that time a great persecution arose against the church which was at Jerusalem; and they were all scattered throughout the regions of Judea and Samaria, except the apostles… Therefore those who were scattered went everywhere preaching the word.

- **You can be, too!!**

3. TO THE END OF THE EARTH

Key Verse 8…"But you shall receive power when the Holy Spirit has come upon you; and you shall be witnesses to Me in Jerusalem, and in all Judea and Samaria, and to the end of the earth."

- To all the earth's inhabitants.
- To the far reaches of the world.
- Until the end of the world/time.

Matt 24:14 And this gospel of the kingdom will be preached in all the world as a witness to all the nations, and then the end will come.

Luke 24:46-47 Then He said to them, "Thus it is written, and thus it was necessary for the Christ to suffer and to rise from the dead the third day, and that repentance and remission of sins should be preached in His name to all nations, beginning at Jerusalem."

Rev 14:6 Then I saw another angel flying in the midst of heaven, having the everlasting gospel to preach to those who dwell on the earth—to every nation, tribe, tongue, and people

- AND THEY DID!
  - Andrew–Asia
  - Peter–Rome
  - John–Asia Minor
  - Thomas–India
  - Paul–Greece, Rome, Spain
- AND WE CAN, TOO!

CONCLUSION

Acts 1:8 But you shall receive power when the Holy Spirit has come upon you; and you shall be witnesses to Me in Jerusalem, and in all Judea and Samaria, and to the end of the earth.

- It takes the power of the Holy Spirit to be a Christian!
- It takes the power of the Holy Spirit to be a witness!

- It takes the power of the Holy Spirit to spread the gospel around the world. Starting in Vinita, going to all Oklahoma, going to all America, then to all the world!

- Do you have this power today?

- Have you received the Holy Spirit since you believed? (Acts 19:2)

- Are you a witness for Jesus?

- How far will you go for him?

- I want to be like Andrew who told his brother Peter about Jesus.

- I want to be like the woman at the well who told her village about Jesus.

- I want to be like the women at the tomb who told others about the risen Lord.

- I want to be like the two on the road to Emmaus who, having seen Jesus personally, went out to tell others that He is alive.

- Have you obeyed Christ's command to receive the power of the Holy Spirit and to be his witness everywhere you go?

John 14:15 "If you love Me, keep My commandments.

Rev 22:14 Blessed are those who do His commandments, that they may have the right to the tree of life, and may enter through the gates into the city.

Now by this we know that we know Him, if we keep His commandments. 4 He who says, I know Him, and does not keep His commandments, is a liar, and the truth is not in him. *1 John 2:3-4*

THE COMMANDS OF CHRIST #16

You Shall Worship The Lord Your God

Matthew 4:10 Then Jesus said to him, "Away with you, Satan!
For it is written, 'You shall worship the Lord your God, and
Him only you shall serve."

John 4:21-24

Jesus said to her, "Woman, believe Me, the hour is coming when you will neither on this mountain, nor in Jerusalem, worship the Father. You worship what you do not know; we know what we worship, for salvation is of the Jews. But the hour is coming, and now is, when the true worshipers will worship the Father in spirit and truth; for the Father is seeking such to worship Him. God is Spirit, and those who worship Him must worship in spirit and truth."

1. WHAT IS WORSHIP?

- Is it a certain method/style?

- Is it a certain day?

- Is it a certain place?

4:21-22 "this mountain" (in Samaria) vs. Jerusalem

- She didn't really worship anywhere.

- It was a religious excuse.

- It was an attempt to distract Jesus from her real issue.

4:24 Jesus was more concerned about worshiping God in spirit and in truth.

- *Worship involves*: Focus on God. Thanksgiving. Praise.

- *Worship includes*: Prayer. Singing. Preaching, etc.

Ps 57:11 (*In a refrain of worship and praise David cried out*) Be exalted, O God, above the heavens; Let Your glory be above all the earth.

Acts 24:14 (*Paul told Felix*) But this I confess to you, that according to the Way which they call a sect, so I worship the God of my fathers, believing all things which are written in the Law and in the Prophets.

Eph 5:17-20 Therefore do not be unwise, but understand what the will of the Lord is. And do not be drunk with wine, in which is dissipation; but be filled with the Spirit, speaking to one another in psalms and hymns and spiritual songs, singing and making melody in your heart to the Lord, giving thanks always for all things to God the Father in the name of our Lord Jesus Christ,

- Do we come to church only for what we get out of it or for what we are to put into it?
- Do you need to learn to worship?

2. WE KNOW WHAT WE WORSHIP

4:22 You worship what you do not know.

Many people perform all that their religion requires, but having never drunk deeply of Him who is the Living Water, their lives are unchanged, dry, and fruitless. Jesus' promise to the woman is universal: Whosoever drinketh of the water that I shall give him shall never thirst; but the water that I shall give him shall be in him a well of water springing up into everlasting life (14). Here it is! Life's superlative offered to a sinful, needy, benighted creature. Outward form is replaced by a new and inner source. Stagnant pools in the soul are transformed into a gushing well. The withered, dead soul of man comes to partake of and participate in "eternal life."

Ye worship ye know not what (22) *The Samaritans rejected all of the Old Testament except the Pentateuch.* Jesus appraisal of the inferiority of their rites and worship is reflected in the use of the neuter pronoun what. *The object of their worship was impersonal, little understood, and vague, not only for the woman but for all in her nation.* There is no such thing as genuine worship based on ignorance or what one does not know. (Beacon)

Acts 17:22-31

Then Paul stood in the midst of the Areopagus and said, "Men of Athens, I perceive that in all things you are very religious; for as I was passing through and considering the objects of your worship, I even found an altar with this inscription:

TO THE UNKNOWN GOD

Therefore, the One whom you worship without knowing, Him I proclaim to you: God, who made the world and everything in it, since He is Lord of heaven and earth, does not dwell in temples made with hands. *Nor is He worshiped with men's hands*, as though He needed anything, since He gives to all life, breath, and all things. And He has made from one blood every nation of men to dwell on all the face of the earth, and has determined their preappointed times and the boundaries of their dwellings, so that they should seek the Lord, in the hope that they might grope for Him and find Him, though He is not far from each one of us; for in Him we live and move and have our being, as also some of your own poets have said, "For we are also His offspring." *Therefore, since we are the offspring of God, we ought not to think that the Divine Nature is like gold or silver or stone, something shaped by art and man's devising.* Truly, these times of ignorance God overlooked, but now commands all men everywhere to repent, because He has appointed a day on which He will judge the world in righteousness by the Man whom He has ordained. He has given assurance of this to all by raising Him from the dead.

4:22 We know what we worship.

- Salvation is not based on a list of do's and don'ts but on a relationship with God through Jesus Christ.

<u>Luke 1:1-4</u> Inasmuch as many have taken in hand to set in order a narrative of those things which have been fulfilled among us (KJV = those things which are most surely believed among us), just as those who from the beginning were eyewitnesses and ministers of the word delivered them to us, it seemed good to me also, having had perfect understanding of all things from the very first, to write to you an orderly account, most excellent Theophilus, that you may know the certainty of those things in which you were instructed.

<u>2 Tim 1:12</u> For I know whom I have believed and am persuaded that He is able to keep what I have committed to Him until that Day.

4:22 For salvation is of the Jews.

Such practices (of worshiping what you do not know) lead either to fanaticism or humanistic legalism. On the other hand, the Jews, with whom Jesus identifies himself, are recognized as the instrument of God's revelation: "We know what we worship; for salvation is of the Jews" (22). (Beacon)

<u>Rom 1:16-17</u> For I am not ashamed of the gospel of Christ, for it is the power of God to salvation for everyone who believes, for the Jew first and also for the Greek. For in it the righteousness of God is revealed from faith to faith; as it is written, "The just shall live by faith."

<u>Gal 3:26-29</u> For you are all sons of God through faith in

Christ Jesus. 2For as many of you as were baptized into Christ have put on Christ. There is neither Jew nor Greek, there is neither slave nor free, there is neither male nor female; for you are all one in Christ Jesus. 2And if you are Christ's, then you are Abraham's seed, and heirs according to the promise.

- Do you know what/whom you worship?

3. TRUE WORSHIPERS

4:23 True worshipers.

- Worshipers of God through Jesus Christ his Son.

Exod. 34:14 (For you shall worship no other God, for the Lord, whose name is Jealous, is a jealous God)

- Based on Commandment #1–Exodus 20:3)
- Christ commanded exclusive worship!

Matt 4:8-10 Again, the devil took Him up on an exceedingly high mountain, and showed Him all the kingdoms of the world and their glory. 9And he said to Him, "All these things I will give You if You will fall down and worship me." Then Jesus said to him, "Away with you, Satan! For it is written, 'You shall worship the Lord your God, and Him only you shall serve.'"

Philippians 2:5-11

Let this mind be in you which was also in Christ Jesus, *who, being in the form of God, did not consider it robbery to be equal with God,* but made Himself of no reputation, taking the form of a bondservant, and coming in the likeness of men. And being found in appearance as a man, He humbled Himself and became obedient to the point of death, even the death of the cross. Therefore God also has highly exalted Him and given Him the name which is above every name, 10 that at the name of Jesus every knee should bow, of those in heaven, and of those on earth, and of those under the earth, and that every tongue should confess that Jesus Christ is Lord, to the glory of God the Father.

Revelation 5:11-14

Then I looked, and I heard the voice of many angels around the throne, the living creatures, and the elders; and the number of them was ten thousand times ten thousand, and thousands of thousands, saying with a loud voice:

"Worthy is the Lamb who was slain
To receive power and riches and wisdom,
And strength and honor and glory and blessing!"
And every creature which is in heaven and on the earth and
under the earth and such as are in the sea,
and all that are in them, I heard saying:

"Blessing and honor and glory and power
Be to Him who sits on the throne,
And to the Lamb, forever and ever!"
Then the four living creatures said, "Amen!"
And the twenty-four elders fell down and
worshiped Him who lives forever and ever.

- False worshippers
  - Do not truly worship God.
  - Do not worship God in Spirit.
  - Do not worship God in truth.

- They worship the devil.
- They worship the things of the world (money, sex, sports, entertainment, etc.)
- They worship humanism and philosophy.

Matt 15:7-9 Hypocrites! Well did Isaiah prophesy about you, saying:

> *"These people draw near to Me with their mouth,*
> *And honor Me with their lips, But their heart is far*
> *from Me. And in vain they worship Me,*
> *Teaching as doctrines the commandments of men."*

John 8:44 You are of your father the devil, and the desires of your father you want to do. He was a murderer from the beginning, and does not stand in the truth, because there is no truth in him. When he speaks a lie, he speaks from his own resources, for he is a liar and the father of it.

- Are you a true worshipper of God?

4. WE MUST WORSHIP GOD IN SPIRIT AND IN TRUTH

4:24 God is Spirit.

- Man is made in the image and likeness of God (Gen 1:17)
- Man is a spirit, clothed with a body.
- The Bible is a spiritual book.

- Christians are spiritual people.

- Heaven is a spiritual place.

<u>Rom 14:17</u> For the kingdom of God is not eating and drinking (not physical), but righteousness and peace and joy in the Holy Spirit (it's spiritual).

4:23-24 But the hour is coming, and now is, when the true worshipers will worship the Father in spirit and truth; for the Father is seeking such to worship Him. 24 God is Spirit, and those who worship Him must worship in spirit and truth.

Now is the time for old forms limited to place and nation to be transformed into a worship that is at once personal, in spirit, and intelligent, in truth. "To worship *in spirit* means that we yield our wills to God's will, our thoughts and plans to God's for us and for the world *in truth* means that we are not worshipping an "Image" of God, made out of our own ideas.

- Our worship must be God-centered.

- Our worship must be spiritual.

- Our worship must be truth-based.

- Do you worship God in spirit and in truth?

CONCLUSION

<u>Matt 4:10</u> Then Jesus said to him, "Away with you, Satan! For it is written, 'You shall worship the Lord your God, and Him only you shall serve.'

<u>John 4:24</u>...God is Spirit, and those who worship Him must worship in spirit and truth."

- The result of the woman at the well's conversation with Jesus is that she was saved and brought a whole town to Christ, and many other were saved..

<u>Rev 22:8-9</u> Now I, John, saw and heard these things. And when I heard and saw, I fell down to worship before the feet of the angel who showed me these things. Then he said to me, "See that you do not do that. For I am your fellow servant, and of your brethren the prophets, and of those who keep the words of this book. Worship God."

DROPPED BY THIS GENERATION

Our fathers suffered to gain us freedom of worship. A later generation heedlessly passes by the open door of the church.

Little Jane said, "Mother, you know that vase you said had been handed down from generation to generation?" "Yes, dear." "Well, Mother, I'm sorry, but this generation has dropped it." (KMB – p.759)

RING IT AGAIN! RING IT AGAIN!

A father once told his son that he was going to take him to visit the country church he used to attend as a boy and where he often rang the bell to call the people to the house of God for worship. Great was their disappointment when they found the old church locked and deserted. Looking through a window they could see the long bell rope. The father borrowed a key and opened the door. The little son looked up into his father's face and eagerly exclaimed, "Father, ring it again! Ring it again!" So once again the old church bell rang out. People came from far and near to see what was the matter. He told them what the church had meant to him in his boyhood, *and with his help the old church was reopened for worship and service in the community.* How we wish that the words of the little boy might resound anew throughout the whole wide world bringing people back to [worship God in spirit and in truth[, "Ring it again! Ring it again!"

- Have you obeyed Christ's command to worship him only?

John 14:15 If you love Me, keep My commandments.

Rev 22:14 Blessed are those who do His commandments, that they may have the right to the tree of life, and may enter through the gates into the city.

And whatever we ask we receive from Him,
because we keep His commandments and do those
things that are pleasing in His sight. *1 John 3:22*

THE COMMANDS OF CHRIST #17

And Him Only You Shall Serve

Matthew 4:10 Then Jesus said to him, "Away with you, Satan! For it is written, 'You shall worship the Lord your God, and Him only you shall serve.'

1. HIM ONLY YOU SHALL SERVE

Key Verse 10…Then Jesus said to him, "Away with you, Satan! For it is written, 'You shall worship the Lord your God, and Him only you shall serve.'

- Many are serving the devil.

- Many are serving idols.

- Many are serving self.

<u>Deut 6:13</u> You shall fear the Lord your God and serve Him.

- Here is man's first and highest duty. (Beacon)

<u>Matt 6:24</u> "No one can serve two masters; for either he will hate the one and love the other, or else he will be loyal to the one and despise the other. You cannot serve God and mammon."

Matthew 17:1-8 *Jesus Only*

Now after six days Jesus took Peter, James, and John his brother, led them up on a high mountain by themselves; and He was transfigured before them. His face shone like the sun, and His clothes became as white as the light. And behold, Moses and Elijah appeared to them, talking with Him. Then Peter answered and said to Jesus, "Lord, it is good for us to be here; if You wish, let us make here three tabernacles: one for You, one for Moses, and one for Elijah." While he was still speaking, behold, a bright cloud overshadowed them; and suddenly a voice came out of the cloud, saying, "This is My beloved Son, in whom I am well pleased. Hear Him!" And when the disciples heard it, they fell on their faces and were greatly afraid. But Jesus came and touched them and said, "Arise, and do not be afraid." 8 When they had lifted up their eyes, they saw no one but Jesus only.

Let Me See Jesus Only – Hymn 451

Let me strive not for the riches Of this earth that soon decay;
From the world I've turned to Jesus
And His more abundant way.
Let me see Jesus only, Jesus only, Jesus only, Le me see Jesus only,
only he can satisfy. (Dr. Dale Oldham)

- Are you serving Jesus only?

(✳)

2. HE CAME TO SERVE

Mark 10:35-45

Then James and John, the sons of Zebedee, came to Him, saying, "Teacher, we want You to do for us whatever we ask." And He said to them, "What do you want Me to do for you?" They said to Him, "Grant us that we may sit, one on Your right hand and the other on Your left, in Your glory." But Jesus said to them, "You do not know what you ask. Are you able to drink the cup that I drink, and be baptized with the baptism that I am baptized with?" They said to Him, "We are able." So Jesus said to them, "You will indeed drink the cup that I drink, and with the baptism I am baptized with you will be baptized; but to sit on My right hand and on My left is not Mine to give, but it is for those for whom it is prepared." And when the ten heard it, they began to be greatly displeased with James and John. But Jesus called them to Himself and said to them, "You know that those who are considered rulers over the Gentiles lord it over them, and their great ones exercise authority over them. *Yet it shall not be so among you; but whoever desires to become great among you shall be your servant.* And whoever of you desires to be first shall be slave of all. For even the Son of Man did not come to be served, but to serve, and to give His life a ransom for many."

Robert K. Greenleaf, founder of the Greenleaf Center for Servant-Leadership in Indianapolis, said, "The great leader is seen as a servant first, and that simple fact is the key to his greatness."

Two thousand years ago, Jesus taught that truth to His disciples and lived it out. As the Son of God, He had been given "all authority...in heaven and on earth" (Matthew 28:18). Yet He did not force people to follow and obey Him. His leadership model was radically different from what we see in today's world. It was one of humility and unselfish service to others.

Servant leaders employ gentle persuasion and reason rather than barking orders and ultimatums.

Whatever our position of leadership, we will never lose it we lose ourselves for others. Service that cares for others is the basis of true greatness. (ODB – 3.16.03)

ONLY THE ONE WHO HAS LEARNED TO SERVE IS QUALIFIED TO LEAD

<u>John 13:12-17</u> So when He had washed their feet, taken His garments, and sat down again, He said to them, "Do you know what I have done to you? 13 You call Me Teacher and Lord, and you say well, for so I am. 14 If I then, your Lord and Teacher, have washed your feet, you also ought to wash one another's feet. *For I have given you an example, that you should do as I have done to you.* Most assuredly, I say to you, a servant is not greater than his master; nor is he who is sent greater than he who sent him. If you know these things, blessed are you if you do them."

- In the ordinance of feetwashing, Jesus teaches humility and servanthood. (Lighthouse – p.66)

God sends His children into the world to shine light on the kingdom of darkness.

None of us is wired to be a servant. Neither were the disciples. But Jesus told His followers that if they served others, God's blessing would be upon them. *Paul links his success in ministry to his servant heart:* "For though I am free from all men, I have made myself a servant to all, that I might win the more." (1 Cor 9:19)

How can you be a "basin bearer and a towel wearer" on your street or in your cul-de-sac? Can you let Jesus' light shine by being a servant among your neighbors?

- Through serving He lost Himself but saved us.
- Through serving we lose ourselves but save others.

Luke 9:23-24 Then He said to them all, "If anyone desires to come after Me, let him deny himself, and take up his cross daily, and follow Me. For whoever desires to save his life will lose it, but whoever loses his life for My sake will save it."

Acts 13:36 (Paul preaches in Antioch in Pisidia) For David, after he had served his own generation by the will of God, fell asleep.

- Are you here to serve or be served?

4. IF YOU WOULD BE GREAT

- The world measures greatness in the number who serve them.
- The Lord measures greatness in the number of people we serve.
- With the Lord, the way up is down.

Jer 45:5 (The LORD said to Baruch) And do you seek great things for yourself? Do not seek them.

Matt 18:1-4 At that time the disciples came to Jesus, saying, "Who then is greatest in the kingdom of heaven?" Then Jesus called a little child to Him, set him in the midst of them, 3 and said, "Assuredly, I say to you, unless you are converted and become as little children, you will by no means enter the kingdom of heaven. Therefore whoever humbles himself as this little child is the greatest in the kingdom of heaven."

Matt 23:11 But he who is greatest among you shall be your servant.

Mark 9:35 And He sat down, called the twelve, and said to them, "If anyone desires to be first, he shall be last of all and servant of all."

Luke 22:27 For who is greater, he who sits at the table, or he who serves? Is it not he who sits at the table? Yet I am among you as the One who serves.

- If you would be great like Jesus, you must serve!

4. OPPORTUNITIES TO SERVE

John 4:35 Do you not say, "There are still four months and then comes the harvest?" Behold, I say to you, lift up your eyes and look at the fields, for they are already white for harvest!

Matthew 25:35-46
For I was hungry and you gave Me food; I was thirsty and you gave Me drink; I was a stranger and you took Me in; I was

naked and you clothed Me; I was sick and you visited Me; I was in prison and you came to Me. Then the righteous will answer Him, saying, "Lord, when did we see You hungry and feed You, or thirsty and give You drink? When did we see You a stranger and take You in, or naked and clothe You? Or when did we see You sick, or in prison, and come to You?" And the King will answer and say to them, "Assuredly, I say to you, inasmuch as you did it to one of the least of these My brethren, you did it to Me." Then He will also say to those on the left hand, "Depart from Me, you cursed, into the everlasting fire prepared for the devil and his angels: for I was hungry and you gave Me no food; I was thirsty and you gave Me no drink; I was a stranger and you did not take Me in, naked and you did not clothe Me, sick and in prison and you did not visit Me.'" Then they also will answer Him, saying, 'Lord, when did we see You hungry or thirsty or a stranger or naked or sick or in prison, and did not minister to You?" Then He will answer them, saying, "Assuredly, I say to you, inasmuch as you did not do it to one of the least of these, you did not do it to Me." And these will go away into everlasting punishment, but the righteous into eternal life."

Jennifer had just heard a disturbing report about an increase in cases of depression among women. The report cited a related upswing in alcoholism and an increased reliance on prescription drugs.

"*So what are You doing about it, Lord?*" Jennifer prayed. But the more she thought about it, the more she felt that God was asking her to do something. All she could see, however, were her own limitations.

To help her think it through, she listed some reasons that were keeping her from action: shyness, fear of getting involved, lack of time, a cold heart, feelings of inadequacy, fear of failure–a daunting list!

As she finished her list, she saw that it was time to pick up her children from school. She put on her coat, then reached for her gloves. They were lying limp and useless–until she slipped her hands inside them. At that moment she realized that God didn't want her to think about her limitations. Rather, He wanted to put His power into her and work through her, just as her gloves became useful when she put her hands into them. (ODB – 9.30.02)

• Are you looking for opportunities to serve??

5. THE NEED IS GREAT
AND GROWING GREATER EVERY DAY!

(ODB – 12.16.02)

Even the weakest among us can participate in sports, but only the strongest can survive as spectators.

According to a heart specialist, when you become a spectator rather than a participant, the wrong things go up and the wrong things go down. Body weight, blood pressure, heart rate, cholesterol, and triglycerides go up. Vital capacity, oxygen consumption, flexibility, stamina, and strength go down.

Being an onlooker in the arena of Christian living is also risky. *The wrong things go up, and the wrong things come down.* Criticism, discouragement, disillusionment, and boredom go up. Sensitivity to sin and the needs of others, and receptivity to the Word of God go down. Sure, there's a certain amount of thrill and excitement in hearing someone's testimony about how God has worked. But it's nothing like knowing that joy yourself. There's no substitute for piling up your own experiences of faith, and using your own God-given abilities in behalf of others.

If we're to be maturing and growing stronger as followers of Jesus Christ, we need to venture out in faith–and that's risky. But remember, it's a far greater risk to be only a spectator.

God call us to get into the game, not to keep the score.

- The need for servants is great!

CONCLUSION

<u>Matthew 4:10</u> Then Jesus said to him, "Away with you, Satan! For it is written, 'You shall worship the Lord your God, and Him only you shall serve.'

1. Are you serving Jesus only?

2. Are you following his example of serving?

3. You must be a servant if you would be great.

4. There are many opportunities to serve.

5. The need for Christian servants is great!

<u>Josh 24:15</u> And if it seems evil to you to serve the Lord, choose for yourselves this day whom you will serve, whether the gods which your fathers served that were on the other side of the River, or the gods of the Amorites, in whose land you dwell. But as for me and my house, we will serve the Lord."

Matt 25:21 His lord said to him, "Well done, good and faithful servant; you were faithful over a few things, I will make you ruler over many things. Enter into the joy of your lord.'"

- Have you obeyed Christ's command to serve Him only?

John 14:15 If you love Me, keep My commandments.

Rev 22:14 Blessed are those who do His commandments, that they may have the right to the tree of life, and may enter through the gates into the city.

By this we know that we love the children of God, when we love God and keep His commandments. 3 For this is the love of God, that we keep His commandments. And His commandments are not burdensome. *1 John 5:2-3*

THE COMMANDS OF CHRIST #18

If You Love Me, Keep My Commandments

John 14:15 If you love Me, keep My commandments.

1. OBEYING CHRIST COMPLETELY

<u>Matthew 28:20 </u>Teaching them to observe all things that I have commanded you.

Genesis 6:8-22

But Noah found grace in the eyes of the Lord. This is the genealogy of Noah. Noah was a just man, perfect in his generations. Noah walked with God. And Noah begot three sons: Shem, Ham, and Japheth. The earth also was corrupt before God, and the earth was filled with violence. So God looked upon the earth, and indeed it was corrupt; for all flesh had corrupted their way on the earth. And God said to Noah, "The end of all flesh has come before Me, for the earth is filled with violence through them; and behold, I will destroy them with the earth. Make yourself an ark of gopherwood; make rooms in the ark, and cover it inside and outside with pitch. And this is how you shall make it: The length of the ark shall be three hundred cubits, its width fifty cubits, and its height thirty cubits. You shall make a window for the ark, and you shall finish it to a cubit from above; and set the door of the ark in its side. You shall make it with lower, second, and third decks. And behold, I Myself am bringing floodwaters on the earth, to destroy from under heaven all flesh in which is the breath of life; everything that is on the earth shall die. But I will establish My covenant with you; and you shall go into the ark—you, your sons, your wife, and your sons' wives with you. And of every living thing of all flesh you shall bring two of every sort into the ark, to keep them alive with you; they shall be male and female. Of the birds after their kind, of animals after their kind, and of every creeping thing of the earth after its kind, two of every kind will come to you to keep them alive. And you shall take for yourself of all food that is eaten, and you shall gather it to yourself; and it shall be food for you and for them." Thus Noah did; according to all that God commanded him, so he did.

Notice that Noah obeyed completely (no instruction was overlooked). (Purpose Driven Life – p.72)

<u>Deut 28:1-2,15</u> Now it shall come to pass, if you diligently obey the voice of the Lord your God, to observe carefully all His commandments which I command you today, that the Lord your God will set you high above all nations of the earth. And all these blessings shall come upon you and overtake you, because you obey

the voice of the Lord your God: But it shall come to pass, if you do not obey the voice of the Lord your God, to observe carefully all His commandments and His statutes which I command you today, that all these curses will come upon you and overtake you.

1 Sam 15:1-23 King Saul fails to obey God's command to completely destroy Amalek

15:3 Now go and attack Amalek, and utterly destroy all that they have, and do not spare them. But kill both man and woman, infant and nursing child, ox and sheep, camel and donkey.

1 Sam 15:1-23 Saul blames the people for sparing the best of the sheep and oxen, and King Agag.

15:22 So Samuel said: "Has the Lord as great delight in burnt offerings and sacrifices, as in obeying the voice of the Lord? Behold, to obey is better than sacrifice, And to heed than the fat of rams.

Jer 7:23-24 But this is what I commanded them, saying, "Obey My voice, and I will be your God, and you shall be My people. And walk in all the ways that I have commanded you, that it may be well with you." Yet they did not obey or incline their ear, but followed the counsels and the dictates of their evil hearts, and went backward and not forward.

Heb 5:8 Though He was a Son, yet He learned obedience by the things which He suffered.

- Have you learned to obey Christ completely?

⟩BEYING CHRIST EXACTLY

⟩ animal population from a worldwide flood required
⟩ion to logistics and details. Everything had to be done
⟩od prescribed it. God didn't say, "Build any old boat
you'd ⟩ke, Noah." He gave very detailed instructions as to the
size, shape, and materials of the ark as well as the different num-
bers of animals to be brought on board. The Bible tells us Noah's
response: "So Noah did everything exactly as God had commanded him."

Notice that Noah obeyed exactly (in the way and time God
wanted it done). (PDL)

Gen 3:1 (that's where Adam and Eve got into trouble) Now the
serpent was more cunning than any beast of the field which the
Lord God had made. And he said to the woman, "Has God indeed said, 'You shall not eat of every tree of the garden'?"

Exod. 25:9,40 (Moses and the Tabernacle – inside and out) According to all that I show you, that is, the pattern of the tabernacle
and the pattern of all its furnishings, just so you shall make it.
And see to it that you make them according to the pattern which
was shown you on the mountain.

Exod. 39:32,43 Thus all the work of the tabernacle of the tent of
meeting was finished. And the children of Israel did according to
all that the Lord had commanded Moses; so they did. Then Moses
looked over all the work, and indeed they had done it; as the Lord
had commanded, just so they had done it..

Chron 28:11-13 (Pattern for the Temple given to David) Then
David gave his son Solomon the plans for the vestibule, its houses, its treasuries, its upper chambers, its inner chambers, and the

place of the mercy seat; and the plans for all that he had by the Spirit, of the courts of the house of the Lord, of all the chambers all around, of the treasuries of the house of God, and of the treasuries for the dedicated things; also for the division of the priests and the Levites, for all the work of the service of the house of the Lord, and for all the articles of service in the house of the Lord.

- Do you think God would fail to plan as diligently for the church?

- Or that he would expect less obedience for all that he expects of the church?

Matt 16:18 And I also say to you that you are Peter, and on this rock I will build My church, and the gates of Hades shall not prevail against it.

- Where there is exact instruction, there must be exact obedience!

Rev 22:18-19 For I testify to everyone who hears the words of the prophecy of this book: If anyone adds to these things, God will add to him the plagues that are written in this book; and if anyone takes away from the words of the book of this prophecy, God shall take away his part from the Book of Life, from the holy city, and from the things which are written in this book.

- His Word/plan needs no improvement.
- His will needs no improvement.
- Have you obeyed Christ exactly?

THE COMMANDS OF CHRIST

3. OBEYING CHRIST WHOLEHEARTEDLY

If God asked you to build a giant boat, don't you think you might have a few questions, objections, or reservations? Noah didn't. He obeyed God wholeheartedly. That means doing whatever God asks without reservation or hesitation...

Often we try to offer God partial obedience. *We want to pick and choose the commands we obey.* We make a list of the commands we like and obey those while ignoring the ones we think are unreasonable, difficult, expensive, or unpopular. I'll attend church but I won't tithe. I'll read my Bible but won't forgive the person who hurt me. *Yet parital obedience is disobedience.*

Wholehearted obedience is done joyfully, with enthusiasm. The Bible says, "Obey him gladly." This is the attitude of David: "Just tell me what to do and I will do it, Lord. As long as I live I'll wholeheartedly obey." (PDL)

- God doesn't want half-hearted or partial obedience.

<u>Num 32:11-12</u> (God told Israel) Surely none of the men who came up from Egypt, from twenty years old and above, shall see the land of which I swore to Abraham, Isaac, and Jacob, because they have not wholly followed Me, except Caleb the son of Jephunneh, the Kenizzite, and Joshua the son of Nun, for they have wholly followed the Lord.

Psalm 119:2, 10, 34, 69, 145

> Blessed are those who keep His testimonies,
> Who seek Him with the whole heart...
> With my whole heart I have sought You;
> Oh, let me not wander from Your commandments...

Give me understanding, and I shall keep Your law; Indeed,
I shall observe it with my whole heart.
The proud have forged a lie against me,
But I will keep Your precepts with my whole heart...
I cry out with my whole heart;
Hear me, O Lord! I will keep Your statutes.

Acts 13:22 David is called "a man after God's own heart" because
he served God with all his heart.

1 Thess 5:23-24 Now may the God of peace Himself sanctify you
completely; and may your whole spirit, soul, and body be preserved blameless at the coming of our Lord Jesus Christ. He who
calls you is faithful, who also will do it.

- "I believe that with *all* my heart!" (Earl Moore)

Christ commands every disciple to spend time with Him and
to hear and obey immediately and thoroughly all He tells us to
do. Jesus said that the disobedient person does not love Him.
(John 14:24). (Lighthouse Devotional – p.61 by Henry Blackaby)

If we want to be lighthouses for Jesus Christ, we will seek out
His commands and joyfully obey them, knowing that obedience
is the key to doing anything for God.

- Have you obeyed Christ whole-heartedly?

4. OBEYING CHRIST WITHOUT RESERVATION OR DELAY

Noah obeyed God without reservation or hesitation. You don't procrastinate and say, "I'll pray about it." You do it without delay. (YES, LORD!) Every parent knows that delayed obedience is really disobedience. *God doesn't owe you an explanation or reason for everything he asks you to do.* Understanding can wait, but obedience can't. Instant obedience will teach you more about God than a lifetime of Bible discussions. In fact, you will never understand some commands until you obey them first. Obedience unlocks understanding. – NOT HOLDING BACK. NOT WAITING. (PDL)

John 2:5 His mother said to the servants, "Whatever He says to you, do it."

Luke 5:4-5 When He had stopped speaking, He said to Simon, "Launch out into the deep and let down your nets for a catch." But Simon answered and said to Him, "Master, we have toiled all night and caught nothing; nevertheless at Your word I will let down the net."

Acts 9:6 So he, trembling and astonished, said, "Lord, what do You want me to do?"

- Not why, but what?

Acts 10:13-14 And a voice came to him, "Rise, Peter; kill and eat." But Peter said, "Not so, Lord! For I have never eaten anything common or unclean." (the woman and the pastor – to become a missionary)

Luke 19:5-6 And when Jesus came to the place, He looked up and saw him, and said to him, "Zacchaeus, make haste and come down, for today I must stay at your house." So he made haste and came down, and received Him joyfully.

 Cor 6:1-2 We then, as workers together with Him also plead with you not to receive the grace of God in vain. For He says: "In an acceptable time I have heard you, And in the day of salvation I have helped you.Behold, now is the accepted time; behold, now is the day of salvation.

- Have you obeyed Christ without reservation or delay?

CONCLUSION

John 14:15 "If you love Me, keep My commandments."

1. Are you obeying Christ completely?
2. Are you obeying Christ exactly?
3. Are you obeying Christ wholeheartedly?
4. Are you obeying Christ without reservation or delay?

Gen 6:22 Thus Noah did; according to all that God commanded him, so he did.

Matt 7:21 Not everyone who says to Me, 'Lord, Lord,' shall enter the kingdom of heaven, but he who does the will of My Father in heaven.

<u>Luke 6:46-49</u> "But why do you call Me "Lord, Lord," and not do the things which I say? Whoever comes to Me, and hears My sayings *and does them*, I will show you whom he is like: He is like a man building a house, who dug deep and laid the foundation on the rock. And when the flood arose, the stream beat vehemently against that house, and could not shake it, for it was founded on the rock.

But he who heard and did nothing is like a man who built a house on the earth without a foundation, against which the stream beat vehemently; and immediately it fell. And the ruin of that house was great.

James, speaking to Christians, said, "We please God by what we do and not only by what we believe. As a child of God you can bring pleasure to your heavenly Father through obedience. *Any act of obedience is also an act of worship.* Why is obedience so pleasing to God? Because it proves you really love him. Jesus said, "If you love me, you will obey my commandments." (Jn. 14:15) (PDL)

Author Eugene Peterson notes that in a culture that loves speed and efficiency, "*it is not difficult…to get a person interested in the message of the gospel; it is terrifically difficult to sustain the interest.*" To follow Christ faithfully, Peterson says, requires "a long obedience in the same direction."

Paul urged the Philippians to adopt the same mindset as Christ, whose obedience to the Father was wholehearted and complete (2:8). He encouraged them to keep on obeying the Lord and to "work out [their] own salvation with fear and trembling" (2:12). (ODB – 2.27.03)

FAITH IN CHRIST IS NOT JUST A SINGLE STEP BUT A LIFE OF WALKING WITH HIM

<u>Rev 22:14</u> Blessed are those who do His commandments, that they may have the right to the tree of life, and may enter through the gates into the city.

This is love, that we walk according to His commandments.
This is the commandment, that as you have heard from the
beginning, you should walk in it. *2 John 6*

THE COMMANDS OF CHRIST #19

Therefore You Also Be Ready

Matthew 24:44 Therefore you also be ready, for the Son of Man is coming at an hour you do not expect.

1. EVERY PERSON NEEDS TO BE READY

Key Verse 44...Therefore you also be ready, for the Son of Man is coming at an hour you do not expect.

Matt 10:29-31 Are not two sparrows sold for a copper coin? And not one of them falls to the ground apart from your Father's will. But the very hairs of your head are all numbered. Do not fear therefore; you are of more value than many sparrows.

- The least person who have ever lived is of far greater value than all the sparrows in the world!

- Christ would have died on the cross if you would have been the only person who ever lived!

<u>Matt 25:31-33</u> When the Son of Man comes in His glory, and all the holy angels with Him, then He will sit on the throne of His glory. All the nations will be gathered before Him, and He will separate them one from another, as a shepherd divides his sheep from the goats. And He will set the sheep on His right hand, but the goats on the left.

- He will come for every person!
- He will gather every person!
- He will judge every person!
- Every king
- Every pauper
- Every citizen of every nation
- Every size, shape, and description of every person
- Every person needs to be ready!

2. THE WORLD NEEDS TO BE READY

Key Verse 44…Therefore you also be ready, for the Son of Man is coming at an hour you do not expect.

<u>Jer 22:29</u> O earth, earth, earth, Hear the word of the Lord! Vvs.19-20…Go therefore and make disciples of all the nations, baptizing them in the name of the Father and of the Son and of the Holy Spirit, 20 teaching them to observe all things that I have commanded you.

John 3:16 For God so loved the world that He gave His only begotten Son, that whoever believes in Him should not perish but have everlasting life.

- The world then

- The world now

- The world of the future

John 4:35 Do you not say, "There are still four months and then comes the harvest?" Behold, I say to you, lift up your eyes and look at the fields, for they are already white for harvest!

- The fields at home–the 80/20 window

- The fields nearby

- The fields abroad–the 10/40 window

- The nearly seven billion people on planet earth!

Rev 14:6 Then I saw another angel flying in the midst of heaven, having the everlasting gospel to preach to those who dwell on the earth—to every nation, tribe, tongue, and people.

- The world needs to be ready!

3. AT DEATH

Key Verse 44…Therefore you also be ready, for the Son of Man is coming at an hour you do not expect.

John 7:6 Then Jesus said to them, "My time has not yet come, but your time is always ready."

John 14:1-3 Let not your heart be troubled; you believe in God, believe also in Me. 2 In My Father's house are many mansions; if it were not so, I would have told you. I go to prepare a place for you. 3 And if I go and prepare a place for you, I will come again and receive you to Myself; that where I am, there you may be also.

John 17:24 Father, I desire that they also whom You gave Me may be with Me where I am, that they may behold My glory which You have given Me.

- Every time a saint of God dies, this prayer of Jesus is answered.
- When facing death, will you say, I've never been ready...
- I used to be ready.
- I hope to be ready.
- I plan to be ready.
- (Sis. Shields) "Always be ready to preach, pray, sing or die!"
- EVERYONE NEEDS TO BE READY AT DEATH!

4. OR AT CHRIST'S COMING

v. 42...Watch therefore, for you do not know what hour your Lord is coming.

Key Verse 44...Therefore you also be ready, for the Son of Man is coming at an hour you do not expect.

- His coming will be *quick*.

<u>Matt 24:27</u> For as the lightning comes from the east and flashes to the west, so also will the coming of the Son of Man be.

- His coming will be *visible.*

<u>Rev 1:7</u> Behold, He is coming with clouds, and every eye will see Him, even they who pierced Him. And all the tribes of the earth will mourn because of Him. Even so, Amen.

- His coming will be *audible.*

<u>2 Peter 3:10</u> But the day of the Lord will come as a thief in the night, in which the heavens will pass away with a great noise, and the elements will melt with fervent heat; both the earth and the works that are in it will be burned up.

- I believe in the "Big Boom" theory of creation. In the beginning, God said, "Let there be light," and *boom* there was light.

- In the end, Jesus will come again, and *boom* the earth and the universe will pass away.

- His coming will be *conclusive.*

<u>Matt 24:14</u> And this gospel of the kingdom will be preached in all the world as a witness to all the nations, and then the end will come.

- There will be no time, no place, no need for a millenial kingdom after Christ comes again.

1 Thessalonians 4:13-18

And now, dear brothers and sisters, we want you to know what will happen to the believers who have died so you will not grieve like people who have no hope. For since we believe that Jesus died and was raised to life again, we also believe that when Jesus returns, God will bring back with him the believers who have died. We tell you this directly from the Lord: We who are still living when the Lord returns will not meet him ahead of those who have died. For the Lord himself will come down from heaven with a commanding shout, with the voice of the archangel, and with the trumpet call of God. First, the Christians who have died will rise from their graves. Then, together with them, we who are still alive and remain on the earth will be caught up in the clouds to meet the Lord in the air. Then we will be with the Lord forever. So encourage each other with these words. (NLT)

Rev 22:20 He who testifies to these things says, "Surely I am coming quickly." Amen. Even so, come, Lord Jesus!

- Everyone needs to be ready at Christ's coming!

CONCLUSION

Matthew 24:44 Therefore you also be ready, for the Son of Man is coming at an hour you do not expect.

1. Are you ready today?
2. Are you concerned about the world being ready?
3. Are you ready to die today?
4. Are you ready for Jesus to come again today?

- Are you as ready as *He* wants you to be?

Matt 25:10 And while they went to buy, the bridegroom came, and those who were ready went in with him to the wedding; and the door was shut.

Rev 19:7 Let us be glad and rejoice and give Him glory, for the marriage of the Lamb has come, and His wife has made herself ready."

As the bride of Christ, we are to make ourselves "ready" for that day by striving to live close to Him now in anticipation of our future with Him in heaven.

1. Jesus, we look forward to that day when we will be with You! We want to be ready, but we know we can't live a life that is pure unless You are in us and help us. Change us and fill us.

- A game we used to play when I was a boy: Hide & Go Seek–"Ready or not, here I come!"

John 14:15 If you love Me, keep My commandments. (ODB – 10.2.13)

Rev 22:14 Blessed are those who do His commandments, that they may have the right to the tree of life, and may enter through the gates into the city.

Blessed are those who do His commandments, that they
may have the right to the tree of life, and may enter through
the gates into the city. *Revelation 22:14*

THE COMMANDS OF CHRIST #20

Be Faithful Until Death, And I Will Give You The Crown Of Life

Revelation 2:10 Do not fear any of those things which you are about to suffer. Indeed, the devil is about to throw some of you into prison, that you may be tested, and you will have tribulation ten days. Be faithful until death, and I will give you the crown of life.

This series has been a Spirit-led attempt to strengthen our understanding of what it means to be a disciple of Christ, and how we can become one.

- Often, during this series, I have mentioned that there are more than twenty commands of Christ. Here is a sample of ten more: _(someone has listed forty nine commands in all)_

1. Let your light so shine before men, that they may see your good works and glorify your Father in heaven. (Matt 5:16)

2. Whoever slaps you on your right cheek, turn the other to him also. (Matt 5:39)

3. Love your enemies, bless those who curse you, do good to those who hate you, and pray for those who spitefully use you and persecute you. (Matt 5:44)

4. Lay up for yourselves treasures in heaven. (Matt 6:20)

5. Therefore do not worry about tomorrow. (Matt 6:34)

6. Judge not, that you be not judged. (Matt 7:1)

7. Ask, and it will be given to you; seek, and you will find; knock, and it will be opened to you. (Matt 7:7)

8. Beware of false prophets, who come to you in sheep's clothing. (Matt 7:15)

9. Watch therefore, for you do not know what hour your Lord is coming. (Matt 24:42)

10. Go out into the highways and hedges, and compel them to come in, that my house may be filled. (Luke 14:23)

1. BE FAITHFUL TO CHRIST

<u>2:10</u> Be faithful until death, and I will give you the crown of life.

- This command came directly from Christ to His church.
- The reward was also to come from Christ.
- Therefore, the need is to be faithful to Christ!
- Not to the pastor

- Not to the church
- But to Christ

Luke 16:10 He who is faithful in what is least is faithful also in much; and he who is unjust in what is least is unjust also in much.

Lam 3:22-23 Through the Lord's mercies we are not consumed,

Because His compassions fail not. They are new every morning; Great is Your faithfulness.

- Great is Your faithfulness, Lord, unto me. I pray that my faithfulness, Lord, will be great unto Thee!

2. BE FAITHFUL TO KEEP HIS COMMANDS

2:10 Be faithful until death, and I will give you the crown of life.

1. Be faithful to seek first the kingdom of God and his righteousness.
2. Be faithful to be born again.
3. Be faithful to repent.
4. Be faithful to receive the Holy Spirit.
5. Be faithful to follow Jesus and become "fishers of men."
6. Be faithful to go & make disciples of all the nations.
7. Be faithful to love one another.
8. Be faithful to deny yourself.

9. Be faithful to forgive.

10. Be faithful to pray.

11. Be faithful to have faith in God.

12. Be faithful to practice the ordinances.

13. Be faithful to do to others as you would have them do to you.

14. Be faithful to give.

15. Be faithful to witness for the Lord.

16. Be faithful to worship the Lord your God.

17. Be faithful to serve only the Lord.

18. Be faithful to keep his commandments.

19. Be faithful to be ready.

20. Be faithful until death.

Key Verse 20…(BE FAITHFUL TO) teach them to observe all things that I have commanded you. (ALL OF THEM!)

3. BE FAITHFUL UNTIL DEATH

2:10 Be faithful until death, and I will give you the crown of life.

Matt 24:13 But he who endures to the end shall be saved.

Mind the Light

Years ago John Walker was the keeper of the light on the Robin's Reef at Staten Island under the United States Government.

There he lived happily in the faithful discharge of his duties for four years. He was then taken with severe pains and Catherine–his wife–sent to the shore for medical help. When this was forthcoming the physician ordered that John should be removed to a hospital at once.

As he was being carried to the boat which was to bear him to the shore he called to his wife, as a parting direction, "Mind the light." He was faithful to his trust to the end.

The poor fellow never returned to the lighthouse. Catherine stayed on to "Mind the light," and carried out the duties so well that she was appointed keeper. Then for more than thirty years she stayed in that lonely spot, caring for the warning beacon to keep mariners from damage on the cruel rocks.

"Mind the light." The words recall for us our duty and privilege as Christians. In the midst of a crooked and perverse generation we are set to "Shine as lights in the world." (KMB – p.201)

<u>Acts 20:24</u> (*Paul told the Ephesian brethren*) But none of these things move me; nor do I count my life dear to myself, so that I may finish my race with joy, and the ministry which I received from the Lord Jesus, to testify to the gospel of the grace of God.

<u>2 Tim 4:6-8</u> For I am already being poured out as a drink offering, and the time of my departure is at hand. I have fought the good fight, I have finished the race, I have kept the faith. Finally, there is laid up for me the crown of righteousness, which the Lord, the righteous Judge, will give to me on that Day, and not to me only but also to all who have loved His appearing.

Faithful to the End

There are those who begin well in the Christian life but who do not "carry through." *It is a joy to see faithfulness maintained to the end.* (The widow of a famous pastor told the following story of her husband) who was taken home to be with the Lord, at seventy-four years of age, after an operation in the hospital.

"On the night before the operation, after the floor nurse had made him comfortable for the night and I went back to his room, he said: 'What do you think has happened?' His face was radiant. 'This dear girl, who has made me comfortable for my night's rest said, as she worked over me: "Dr. Jenness, I'm a good girl, and I go to church and Sunday School when I can get away from my work, but I'm not a Christian. Can you tell me how to be one?"

And then he said: 'I had her hand me my Bible, and I read some passages to her and prayed with her, and gave her several little tracts that were in my handbag, and she has promised to read them, and I'll talk with her again when I'm better.'

'Valiant'—yes, valiant to the end for the Lord he loved so dearly and served so faithfully. I stood by his bed and held his dear hand till he entered the gates of the city that hath foundations, whose builder and maker is God!" (KMB – p.201)

4. AND HE WILL GIVE YOU THE CROWN OF LIFE

<u>2:10</u> Be faithful until death, and I will give you the crown of life.
- Crown of life: life everlasting, heaven;, eternal reward, etc.

<u>Isa 33:17</u> Your eyes will see the King in His beauty; They will see the land that is very far off.

1 Cor 9:25 And everyone who competes for the prize is temperate in all things. Now they do it to obtain a perishable crown, but we for an imperishable crown.

Jas. 1:12 Blessed is the man who endures temptation; for when he has been approved, he will receive the crown of life which the Lord has promised to those who love Him.

1 Peter 5:2-4 Shepherd the flock of God which is among you, serving as overseers, not by compulsion but willingly, not for dishonest gain but eagerly; nor as being lords over those entrusted to you, but being examples to the flock; and when the Chief Shepherd appears, you will receive the crown of glory that does not fade away.

Rev 3:11 Behold, I am coming quickly! Hold fast what you have, that no one may take your crown.

Rev 4:4 Around the throne were twenty-four thrones, and on the thrones I saw twenty-four elders sitting, clothed in white robes; and they had crowns of gold on their heads.

CONCLUSION

Matthew 24:44 Therefore you also be ready, for the Son of Man is coming at an hour you do not expect."

1. Be faithful to Christ
2. Be faithful to keep all his commands

3. Be faithful to death

4. And he will give you the crown of life

1 Cor 4:2 Moreover it is required in stewards that one be found faithful.

- **How to be a world-class Christian**: Make a great commitment to the Great Commandment, and to the Great Commission.

Matt 28:19 Go therefore and make disciples of all the nations, baptizing them in the name of the Father and of the Son and of the Holy Spirit,

Key Verse 20…"teaching them to observe all things that I have commanded you; and lo, I am with you always, even to the end of the age." Amen.

- Which Commands of Christ do you have trouble with?
- Are you observing and keeping *all* of them?
- A person who claims to be a Christian but does not follow the example of Christ and keep His commandments is deceiving himself. (Daily Bible – p.523)
- The Commands of Christ lead us to salvation.
- The Commands of Christ lead us to full discipleship.
- The Commands of Christ will lead us to heaven.

John 14:15 If you love Me, keep My commandments.

Rev 22:14 Blessed are those who do His commandments, that they may have the right to the tree of life, and may enter through the gates into the city.

- If we do not obey Christ's "Great Commission" it will become the "Great Omission!"
- We must observe all things that He has commanded us!
- We must teach others to observe all things that He has commanded us.
- This is how we make disciples.
- This is how we create a healthy church.

THE ABC'S OF SALVATION

"For God so loved the world that He gave His only begotten Son, that whoever believes in Him should not perish but have everlasting life." John 3:16

Receiving Jesus Christ is as simple as A-B-C...

A – ADMIT THAT YOU HAVE SINNED. "for all have sinned and fall short of the glory of God." Romans 3:23

B – BELIEVE THAT JESUS CHRIST DIED FOR YOU. "But as many as received Him, to them He gave the right to become children of God, even to those who believe in His name." John 1:12

C – CONFESS THAT JESUS CHRIST IS LORD OF YOUR LIFE. "that if you confess with your mouth the Lord Jesus and believe in your heart that God has raised him from the dead, you will be saved. For with the heart one believes to righteousness, and with the mouth confession is made to salvation." Romans 10:9-10

The Bible says that you may know sure that you're saved (1 John 5:13). If you wish to receive Christ as your Lord and Savior, then pray the following "Sinner's Prayer:" "Dear Lord Jesus, I know that I am a sinner. I believe that You died for my sins and arose from the grave. I now turn from my sins and invite You to come into my heart and life. I receive You as my personal Savior and follow You as my Lord. Amen."

If you prayed to receive Christ as your Savior please sign your name and date below when you made this decision (that helps to make it final) and be sure to tell someone. You may contact any pastor and tell them of your decision to receive Christ as your Savior.

Name:_____ Date:_____

————————(✳)————————